Two week
loan

Please return on or before the last
date stamped below.
Charges are made for late return.

IS 239/0799

INFORMATION SERVICES PO BOX 430, CARDIFF CF10 3XT

ORGANISATIONAL PROSECUTIONS

To Suzanne, Hannah, Emily and Charlotte

Organisational Prosecutions

GARY SLAPPER
The Open University

Ashgate

DARTMOUTH

Aldershot • Burlington USA • Singapore • Sydney

Published by
Dartmouth Publishing Company
Ashgate Publishing Limited
Gower House
Croft Road
Aldershot
Hants GU11 3HR
England

Ashgate Publishing Company
131 Main Street
Burlington, VT 05401-5600 USA

Ashgate website: http://www.ashgate.com

British Library Cataloguing in Publication Data
Slapper, Gary
    Organisational prosecutions
    1. Criminal justice, Administration of - England 2. Criminal
    justice, Administration of - Wales
    I. Title
    345.4'2

Library of Congress Control Number: 2001091687

ISBN 0 7546 2059 X

Printed and bound in Great Britain by Antony Rowe Ltd.,
Chippenham, Wiltshire.

Contents

List of Tables

Table of Legislation

Acknowledgements

I am deeply indebted to Suzanne, Hannah, Emily and Charlotte for their patience and understanding while I was writing, and to David and Julie Whight and Doreen and Ivor Slapper for bearing burdens beyond the normal call of grandparenthood. I would like to thank OUBS Research Associate Marilyn Lannigan for her excellent work in collecting and classifying the empirical data from the Magistrates' Courts at Newcastle-under-Lyme, Milton Keynes and Horseferry Road in London. The work she conducted in the Law Library was also magnificent. The project enjoyed a great benefit through her tireless professionalism, punctiliousness and patience. I would like to acknowledge the excellent statistical and analytical work of Claire Simpson without whose observant eye and technical know-how this research would have been greatly weakened.

Thanks are also due to the Open University Business School Research Committee for supporting this research, and to the Magistrates' Courts and Justices Clerks at the courthouses for their kind permission to examine the Court Registers. I am very grateful for the kind cooperation of Mrs G. Houghton-Jones, Justices' Clerk at Horseferry Road Magistrates' Court, to Mrs Susan Lutter, Clerk to the Justices at Milton Keynes Magistrates' Court, and to Mr M.P. Benson, Clerk to the Justices in the North Staffordshire Magistrates' Courts. I would also like to thank all the Justices' Clerks who took the time to answer the questionnaire (presented in Appendix 3) and to contribute some very helpful observations.

Preface

The focus of this text is an area of activity with neither a name nor a social recognition that it exists as such. After much reading, deliberation and discussion with officials within the court structure, lawyers and legal academics, I settled on the title of *Organisational Prosecutions* because it was the form of words which came closest to the precise subject of the book without having to use 20 words, a colon and several commas. The theme is the activity of the multifarious agencies, local and central governmental departments, private companies, and organisations which act as prosecutors in that branch of the criminal justice system which deals with 95 per cent of all offences, the magistrates' courts.

There is a lot going on in this unlabelled process of the criminal justice system. There are over 30 prosecuting organisations (21 are featured in this text) which act regularly in over 400 courthouses in England and Wales. This activity, involving very many people and a good deal of resources, accounts for something like one-fifth of activity in the criminal courts, yet almost no research has been conducted in this area. The only other significant study was conducted over 20 years ago before several major changes in the legal system that were introduced in the 1980s and 1990s.

Following alleged electoral irregularities, the world had to wait longer than it expected for the final result of the 43rd American Presidential election. It is worth noting, however, that as soon as it became apparent that there was a problem in the counting of votes cast in Florida, one of the Presidential candidates had 75 lawyers put on a plane to the state within the hour.

At the forefront of all law is criminal law. There are probably two reasons for this. One is that the operation of all branches of law depends, ultimately, on enforcement from the criminal law, i.e. anyone subject to a civil court order or request to pay compensation, or a family court order will ultimately face imprisonment if he or she refuses to recognise the legitimacy of the legal system. The second reason for criminal law being at the forefront of all law is that, unlike the law of probate, the law of trusts or town planning law, it governs the sort of conduct of which dramatic stories are made (violence, robbery, sex, drugs etc.) and can be made accessible to most citizens. The significance of this last point has not been lost on governments over the centuries. Many administrations have been aware of the need to manage criminal law in a way that either terrorises the citizenry to such an extent that disorder is kept at bay through judicial and penological tyranny, or, as is the more modern way, builds support for the legal system as a whole by being accepted as fair in the way it identifies and prosecutes suspects, and punishes offenders.

According to a recent document from the Home Office, the criminal justice system costs £12 billion per year to operate. The same document gives, as an estimate of the cost of a substantive court proceeding in a magistrates' court, the figure of £550. This means that the total cost of the 9,689 cases looked at in this book is £5,328,950. That figure is probably an overestimate because, although some of the cases in the study were protracted and would have cost more than £550, many of the cases in this study were matters concerning offences like not having a television licence, which would have cost less than £550 to process. None the less, in very general terms, if the cases prosecuted by organisations other than the Crown Prosecution Service in 1998 at three magistrates' courts cost about £5 million, then it is safe to say that the total cost incurred across 350 other magistrates' courts would have been over £550 million for the same year. Despite the facts that the multifarious prosecuting organisations are all using the same rules of evidence and procedure, are bringing their cases in the same forum (the magistrates' court), and are subjecting their defendants to the same possible punishments, they have no umbrella system under which they operate.

Since 1 January 1986, most prosecutions are brought by the Crown Prosecution Service but there are still so many brought by other organisations that this area deserves much closer attention than it has hitherto received.

Chapter One

Research Methodology, Statistical Technique and Findings

In this chapter I set out the research methodology used in the project, and explain some of the main statistical assumptions on which the work is based. It is convenient here to use explanations of the statistical methods to also demonstrate some of the research findings.

The main purposes of this research were:

1) to discover which non-CPS agencies were commonly prosecuting in magistrates' courts;
2) to discover the extent of such prosecutions;
3) to examine possible different patterns of non-CPS cases in respect of different types of magistrates' court;
4) to evaluate the effectiveness and efficiency of the respective agencies in bringing such prosecutions;
5) to identify and assess the implications of these findings in relation to public policy on criminal justice matters.

Information concerning non-CPS prosecutions is collected and categorised neither centrally nor at individual courts. For this reason the only way to conduct this research was to go to specific magistrates' courts and to trawl laboriously through all of the court Registers picking out those prosecutions which were not brought by the Crown Prosecution Service. The three magistrates' courts selected for the purposes of this study – Milton Keynes, Horseferry Road London, and Newcastle-under-Lyme – were chosen in order to represent a range of courts.

Milton Keynes is a large new town in Buckinghamshire with a population of 200,000. In 1967 the Minister of Housing and Local Government designated 22,000 acres in the Buckinghamshire countryside to be used for the development of a new town. The area included the existing towns of Bletchley, Stony Stratford, Wolverton, Olney, and New Bradwell, along with many villages. Milton Keynes is now a growing centre of light industry and many new company head offices. The town is served by a grid of roads designed for cars and lorries as opposed to much of the road network serving older towns and cities where roadways cut in a different age have been adapted for use by a high throughput of modern vehicles.

Horseferry Road magistrates' court is a busy court in Central London. It sits in South Westminster Petty Sessional Area (PSA) – the third largest PSA in England and Wales. Its weighted caseload is 102,693 for the calendar year 1999 but the court expects to have a higher caseload in future years, based on current trends. It covers the heart of the West End of London. Its resident population is increased daily by the influx of commuters and tourists that is reflected in the varied nature of the court work. As well as dealing with the full range of criminal activities, the court also has responsibility for Betting and Gaming and Liquor Licensing for the whole of Westminster, out of hours applications related to the Police and Criminal Evidence Act 1984 and also hosts the Psychiatric Liaison Service for Westminster and West London.

The Borough of Newcastle-under-Lyme is centrally located between Manchester and Birmingham with a population of just over 123,000. Its name dates back to the 12th century when, during a period of civil and political upheaval, a castle was founded to command the strategically important junction where the route running north from London to Carlisle split off west to Chester. The area now occupied by the Borough of 81 square miles formed part of a huge forest of lime trees which covered most of northwest Staffordshire at that time.

Staffordshire Magistrates' Court Service serves a population of 1,054,380 and operates from 10 court houses and six administrative centres. Newcastle-under-Lyme Magistrates' Court has five court rooms and of the 607 magistrates on the Staffordshire Commission as at 31 March 1999, 77 were assigned to Newcastle-under-Lyme with a total of 3,193 court sitting hours (North Staffordshire Magistrates' Courts Committee, 1998/99).

The data collected for each of the three courts in this study were those relating to court business of 1998, and were collected throughout 1999.

Information about the cases was gathered under the headings: the date and number of the case; the name of the informant; the nature of the offence; the statute under which the offence was being prosecuted; the plea; the verdict; the disposal; whether the defendant was present in court; and whether the defendant was represented. This last datum was filled in on the court registers only at the discretion of the court official recording the information, and was not available, in fact, in the majority of cases.

In order to facilitate the collation of data, a Prosecution Questionnaire designed to be used with the SNAP system was designed and used at each court (see Appendix 3). This questionnaire enabled information gathered from the court Registers to be quickly put into helpful categories.

Overall, throughout the three courts, information was gathered on 9,689 cases.

In addition to this quantitative information gathering, it was thought appropriate to collect, analyse and evaluate the opinions of magistrates' Court Clerks (the legal advisors to lay Justices of the Peace). To that end, 100 magistrates' courts were sent a questionnaire (Appendix 3) seeking their opinions on this part of the workings of the Criminal Justice System, and giving them an opportunity to submit a statement. There was a 68 per cent response rate, and many of the response statements were encouragingly detailed and thoughtful.

Summary of Statistical Findings from the Prosecution Survey

Tests of Significance for the Relationship between the Variables: Court and Prosecutor

- First, it should be noted that we are dealing with categorical data. A categorical variable is one for which the measurement scale consists of a set of categories. For example 'Horseferry Road', 'Milton Keynes' and 'Newcastle Under Lyme'. There are two forms of categorical data – ordinal and nominal. Ordinal figures denote a thing's position in a sequence or series. We are dealing, however, with nominal data – nominal scales are made up of numbers, but these numbers do not stand in any particular relationship to each other and cannot be used to perform arithmetic. For nominal variables, the order of listing the categories is irrelevant, and the statistical analysis should not depend on that ordering.
- With this in mind we cannot perform measures of central tendency or calculations of variance. The appropriate statistic to use is a chi-square. It should be noted that a chi-square is not a strong statistic in that it does not convey information about the strength of the relationship. The combination of contingency table and chi-square is most likely to occur when either both variables are nominal (categorical) or when one is nominal and the other ordinal.

- An overall chi-square test was carried out to ascertain at the most simple level that there was a significant association between the proportion of prosecutions brought about and the three courts. To understand fully this relationship further chi-square tests were carried out.
- Chi-square tests were carried out on three-by-two contingency tables to test the null hypothesis that there is no difference in the proportion of prosecutions brought about by a particular agency in the three courts (see Table 1.1).

  It should be noted that a significant result can be interpreted as follows, there is a statistically significant difference in the proportion of prosecutions brought about by the relevant prosecutor (e.g. DVLA) in the three different courts. In each case a two by three contingency table has been used to analyse the data and, comparing individual frequencies, one can then establish which differences are most significant. For the purposes of the present analysis the data has not been further subdivided into two by two tables as it is clear where the differences lie.

  When a result is found not to be significant we are not denying the proportional differences, we are merely stating that the chi-square value is not large enough for us to be confident that this could not have arisen by chance.

- Next, using chi-square, we analysed tables with three rows (representing the three courts) and several columns for the difference types of offence prosecuted by a particular agency. In each case, we tested the null hypothesis that the proportion of people prosecuted for any individual offence brought about by a particular agency does *not* differ significantly between the three courts. Even if the null hypothesis is true, this does not preclude differences between any selected two-by-two combinations of the data, for example that the proportion of drivers prosecuted for obstructing a police officer was significantly different between the three courts, though this is more a reflection of the low cell counts than a dependent relationship. The resultsobtained are shown in Table 1.2.

  To summarise by using the example of the DVLA:

STEP 1: The question: 'is there a significant difference in the *proportion* of prosecutions brought about by the DVLA between the three courts?' can be answered: 'Yes', as examination of the chi-square statistic shows that the $p<0.001$. In this example the differences in the proportions can be established by looking at the results, that is,

7/3211 is clearly a much smaller proportion than 1862/5226 – none the less the statistical significance has been established.

Table 1.1   Relationship between court and prosecutor

Relationship between the court and prosecutor	Is the difference statistically significant at 1% level?	Comment
DT/DVLA	Yes	
Vehicle inspectorate	Yes	
TVLEO	Yes	
Environment Agency	Yes	
Electricity	No	All cases are in Newcastle-under-Lyme hence no differences to report
DSS	Yes	
RSPCA	No	
DTI	Yes	One cell has expected count less than five
Trading Standards	Yes	One cell has expected count less than five
Education Welfare	Yes	One cell has expected count less than five
British Waterways	No	All cases are in Milton Keynes, hence no differences to report
BT Security	No	All cases are in Milton Keynes, hence no differences to report
Inland Revenue		All cases are in Milton Keynes, hence no differences to report
Customs & Excise	Yes	
HSE	Yes	Two cells have expected count less than five
SW Trains		All cases are at Horseferry Road, hence no differences to report
Cab Law Enforcement		All cases are at Horseferry Road, hence no differences to report
London Buses		All cases were at Horseferry Road, hence no differences to report
Department of Health	No	Only one case
Borough/County Councils	No	
Ministry of Agriculture	No	Only one case

Table 1.2 Proportion of offences prosecuted in the courts

Was there a significant difference in the proportion of people prosecuted for any individual offence between the agency and the three courts?		Comment
DT/DVLA	No	
Vehicle inspectorate	Yes	19 cells have a count less than five
TVLEO	No	
Environment Agency	No	Non computable as only one offence specified by agency
Electricity	No	9 cells have a count less than five
DSS	Yes	9 cells have a count less than five
RSPCA	No	Non computable as only one offence specified by agency
DTI	Yes	17 cells have a count less than five
Trading Standards	Yes	10 cells have a count less than five
Education Welfare	No	Non computable as only one offence specified by agency
British Waterways	No	Non computable as only one offence specified by agency
BT Security	No	Non computable as only one offence specified by agency
Inland Revenue	No	Non computable as only one court specified
Customs & Excise	Yes	3 cells have a count less than five
HSE	Yes	4 cells have a count less than five
SW Trains	No	Non computable as only one court and one offence specified
Cab Law Enforcement	No	Non computable as only one court specified
London Buses	No	Non computable as only one court and one offence specified
Department of Health	No	Only one case
Borough/County Councils	Yes	77 cells have a count less than five
Ministry of Agriculture	No	Non computable as only one court and one offence specified

Table 1.3   Prosecutions brought about by the DVLA

	DVLA	Non-DVLA	Total
Horseferry Road	7	3,204	3,211
Milton Keynes	1,862	3,364	5,226
Newcastle-under-Lyme	451	801	1,252
Total	2,320	7,369	9,689

STEP 2:

Table 1.4   Individual offences prosecuted by the DVLA

	Total DVLA	Driver and vehicle licence offences	No trade/ goods licence	Obstructing a police officer
Horseferry Road	7	7	0	0
Milton Keynes	1,862	1,851	11	0
Newcastle-under-Lyme	451	450	0	1
Total	2,320	2,308	11	1

Having established that a relationship exists between the proportion of prosecutions brought about by the DVLA and the different courts we now ask a second question: 'Are there significant differences in the *proportion* of individual offences prosecuted by the DVLA among the three courts?' The answer is 'No' as the differences were not significantly different.

As can been clearly seen from the chi-square analysis in the case of DVLA, the null hypothesis is accepted and we conclude that the proportion of drivers prosecuted for an individual driving offence brought about by the DVLA does not differ significantly between the three courts. However, on examination of the full contingency table above it can be seen that there are marked differences in individual frequencies and further analysis can establish that these are significant.

Where a significant result appears, we can look at the residuals. The largest residuals are associated with the cells that contribute most to the chi-square statistic. All residuals larger than two in magnitude show significant discrepancies between what is expected and what is observed.

Identification of Other Relationships within the Data

First, we should look at the frequencies for the variables:

Table 1.5   Frequency of case results

Verdict	Frequency	Per cent	Valid per cent	Cumulative per cent
Convicted/proved	6,555	67.7	67.7	67.7
Not guilty	6	.1	.1	67.7
Withdrawn/dismissed	1,047	10.8	10.8	78.5
Adjourned	1,343	13.9	13.9	92.4
Warrant issued for arrest	47	.5	.5	92.9
Summons not served	358	3.7	3.7	96.6
Remanded in custody	81	.8	.8	97.4
Remanded on bail	251	2.6	2.6	100.0
Total	9,688	100.0	100.0	100.0
Missing from system	1	.0		
Total	9,689	100.0		

Our attention was drawn to the fact that the frequency for those found 'not guilty' is very small – only six people. With this in mind the 'verdict' variable was re-coded to 'not guilty' or 'other' (other includes all categories other than guilty). This gave the following frequencies:

Table 1.6   Frequency of verdicts

Guilty		Frequency	Per cent	Valid per cent	Cumulative per cent
Valid	Other	3,113	32.3	32.3	32.3
	Guilty	6,555	67.7	67.7	100.0
	Total	9,688	100.0	100.0	
Missing from system		1	.0		
Total		9,689	100.0		

Similarly the variable 'plea' was re-coded so that 'guilty' and 'guilty MCA' were summed and 'not guilty' and 'not guilty MCA' were summed ('guilty MCA' throughout the text means that the defendant pleaded guilty by post as permitted by the Magistrates' Court Act 1980 s.12 as substituted by Schedule

5 to the Criminal Justice and Public Order Act 1994. This created a new variable 'plea1' with the following frequencies:

Table 1.7   Frequency of verdicts and outcomes

Plea1		Frequency	Per cent	Valid per cent	Cumulative per cent
Valid	Guilty	2,548	26.3	26.3	26.3
	Not guilty	383	4.0	4.0	30.3
	No appearance	4,805	49.6	49.6	79.9
	Not known	1,593	16.4	16.4	96.3
	N/A	359	3.7	3.7	100.0
	Total	9,688	100.0	100.0	
Missing from system		1	.0		
Total		9,689	100.0		

Relationship between 'Plea' and 'Guilty' Verdict

- Of those that were found guilty the largest proportion were those that 'did not appear in court' (55 per cent). The next largest group, not surprisingly, were those that pleaded 'guilty' (36 per cent). Only 2 per cent of those that were found guilty had pleaded 'not guilty'.
- Of those that pleaded 'guilty' it is not surprising that 92 per cent were found guilty! The remaining 8 per cent of cases can be accounted for as cases in which the prosecution failed for some procedural reason, were discontinued, or where a decision was still pending.
- Similarly, of those that pleaded 'not guilty', 25 per cent were found guilty in comparison to 75 per cent who pleaded 'not guilty'.
- Of those that 'made no appearance', 75 per cent were found guilty.

If we filter the cases to produce a direct comparison between those who pleaded 'guilty' and those who pleaded 'not guilty', we find that:

- of those that were found guilty 96 per cent had pleaded guilty;
- of those found 'not guilty' 58 per cent had pleaded 'not guilty' in comparison with 42 per cent who pleaded 'guilty'.

All the above relationships were tested to be statistically significant at the 1 per cent level.

We conclude that there is *inter alia* a relationship between what the defendant pleas and whether they were found to be guilty. However, at this stage we can say nothing about the causality of these relationships. We need, therefore, to carry out a logistic regression in order to establish which of the factors has the most significant 'impact' or effect on the dependent variable: whether or not the defendant is found guilty.

Relationship between 'Whether the Accused was Present in Court' and 'Guilty Verdict'

- Of those found guilty, 74 per cent of them were not in court.
- Of those found not guilty, 44 per cent were not in court.
- Of those who were present in court, 55 per cent were found guilty and 45 per cent not guilty.
- Of those not present in court 78 per cent were found guilty and 22 per cent not guilty.

All the above relationships were tested to be statistically significant at the 1 per cent level.

Relationship between 'Whether the Accused was Represented in Court' and 'Guilty Verdict'

- Of those found guilty, 2 per cent were represented in court, 24 per cent were not represented, but for 75 per cent as the information was not on the court record, we do not know whether or not they were represented in court.
- Of those found not guilty, 3 per cent were represented in court, 5 per cent were not represented, but for 81 per cent we do not know if they were represented in court, and for 11 per cent the question was not applicable.
- Of those represented in court, 57 per cent were found guilty and 43 per cent found not guilty.
- Of those not represented in court, 90 per cent were found guilty and 10 per cent found not guilty.

Relationship between 'Which Court they Attended' and 'Guilty Verdict'

- Of those defendants found guilty, 30 per cent of them were prosecuted at

Horseferry Road, 56 per cent of them from Milton Keynes and 14 per cent at Newcastle-under-Lyme.

- Of those found not guilty, 40 per cent of them were prosecuted at Horseferry Road, 49 per cent of them at Milton Keynes and 11 per cent at Newcastle-under-Lyme.
- Of those prosecuted at Horseferry Road, 61 per cent were found guilty and 39 per cent found not guilty.
- Of those prosecuted at Milton Keynes, 71 per cent were found guilty and 29 per cent found not guilty.
- Of those prosecuted at Newcastle-under-Lyme, 72 per cent were found guilty and 28 per cent found not guilty.

All the above relationships were tested to be statistically significant at the 1 per cent level.

Relationship between Verdict and Disposal

It is not possible to calculate a measure of association for this relationship since one of the variables is a constant – that is the relationship we are examining is that of 'being found guilty' (constant) and what was the disposal (i.e. the sentence given). This provides the frequencies set out in Table 1.8.

Relationship between the Prosecuting Body and Being Found Guilty

The relationship between who the prosecuting body was and being found guilty is best shown in a tabular form (Table 1.9). All relationships are statistically significant at the 1 per cent level.

The above table provides a crude comparison of the 'success' of the individual prosecuting bodies at bringing about a guilty verdict. This can be advanced only as a crude indication since we must remember that for some of the organisations we are dealing with very small numbers (only one case for the Ministry of Agriculture and the Department of Health).

Alternatively, we can also consider what proportion of those that were found guilty belong to a particular prosecuting body, again this is best shown in a tabular form (Table 1.10). All relationships are statistically significant at the 1 per cent level.

Cells where per cent is left blank indicate that the percentage was less than 0.1 per cent.

Table 1.8   Convictions and disposals

		Frequency	Per cent	Valid per cent	Cumulative per cent
Valid	Fine	6,146	63.4	93.8	93.8
	Remanded on bail	126	1.3	1.9	95.7
	Remanded in custody	5	.1	.1	95.8
	Imprisonment	14	.1	.2	96.0
	Probation	22	.2	.3	96.3
Community Service		56	.6	.9	97.2
Combination order		8	.1	.1	97.3
Absolute discharge		80	.8	1.2	98.5
Conditional discharge		95	1.0	1.4	100.0
Sentence suspended		2	.0	.0	100.0
Total		6,554	67.6	100.0	

Table 1.9   Case outcomes by agency

	Not guilty	Guilty
DT/DVLA	20%	80%
Vehicle inspectorate	33%	67%
TVLEO	29%	71%
Environment Agency	26%	74%
Electricity	72%	28%
DSS	59%	41%
RSPCA	72%	28%
DTI	87%	13%
Trading Standards	46%	54%
Education Welfare	35%	65%
British Waterways	10%	90%
BT Security	25%	75%
Inland Revenue	99%	1%
Customs & Excise	88%	12%
HSE	53%	47%
SW Trains	30%	70%
Cab Law Enforcement	17%	83%
London Buses	30%	70%
Department of Health	100%	
Borough/County Councils	31%	69%
Ministry of Agriculture	100%	

Table 1.10   Proportion of guilty verdicts belonging to the different agencies

	Not guilty	Guilty
DT/DVLA	15%	28%
Vehicle inspectorate	6%	6%
TVLEO	9%	10%
Environment Agency	1%	1%
Electricity	0.4%	0.1%
DSS	10%	3%
RSPCA	0.6%	0.1%
DTI	1%	0.1%
Trading Standards	0.5%	0.3%
Education Welfare	1%	1%
British Waterways	%	0.1%
BT Security	%	%
Inland Revenue	7%	0%
Customs & Excise	3%	0.2%
HSE	0.3%	0.1%
SW Trains	3%	3%
Cab Law Enforcement	%	0.1%
London Buses	4%	5%
Department of Health	%	
Borough/County Councils	39%	42%
Ministry of Agriculture	%	

Clearly, the above examples serve to illustrate the complexities of establishing relationships using chi-square. Moreover, as previously stated, in order fully to understand this relationship we need to carry out multivariate analysis.

Multivariate Analysis

This analysis entails the proposition that all regression involves association but not is not conclusive of causation.

Log Linear Analysis

Log linear analysis follows a pattern of thought more nearly akin to tabular analysis and chi-squared, using one of the mathematical transformations which render data more nearly 'normal' in the statistical sense. An expected value is computed for every cell of the table and all possible effects (row differences, column differences, differences between blocks, interaction effects) on the presumption that all the effects are zero and the cases are randomly distributed. Differences from this null hypothesis can be tested. A series of chi-squared statistics is often used to test the significance of any observable differences or correlations, and the results may be presented in a form similar to the output from an analysis of variance.

The data themselves may be presented as raw figures, percentages, proportions, rates or *odds ratios*.

Odds ratios – comparative data are sometimes represented, particularly in logistic regression, in the form of odds ratios – the ratio of two probabilities. For example, if 20 per cent of men in a sample were found guilty and but only 5 per cent of women, we would say that the odds of being found guilty are 4:1 if you are a man and 19:1 if you are a woman. The ratio of these two figures is $^1/_4/^1/_{19}$ = 4.75 and this is the odds ratio. It may be interpreted as meaning that you are a little less than five times more likely to be found guilty if you are a male than if you are a female.

The power of the technique for survey analysis and theory testing is that it will allow us to build a model specifying which effects ought to be significant and to see by how much these predict different results from the null hypothesis of no association, to see how well the model fits the observed data and to compare the performance of different models.

Logistic Regression

The general log linear model will accommodate variables with any number of categories and does not posit independent and dependent variables; it is used to explain all the variance in the figures, privileging one variable as dependent by the researcher's choice of interaction models. The most used version for survey analysis, however, logistic regression, is a hybrid between log linear and regression analysis and is used for explaining variance in a dependent variable which is expressed in the form of a dichotomy – e.g. 'guilty' or 'not guilty'.

The logistic regression used here depends upon the notion of calculating the odds – probabilities – of a given case lying in one rather than the other of the two categories of the dependent variable. The logit is the logarithm of the odds or probabilities. Probabilities form an interval level variable and can therefore be used in a form of regression which assesses how much a given variable contributes in terms of lengthening or shortening the odds of belonging to a given category. This form of analysis will then produce tests of significance of the overall effect and also of each single variable and of their interactions. The test involved is generally a version of chi-square, comparing the observed distribution of the independent variable with the distribution predicted on the basis of the independents variables.

The great analytic strengths of all log linear analysis are that: a) it works on categorical (nominal) data – more common in survey research than any other kind; and b) that it will allow one to test the fit of different hypotheses to the data.

Logistic Regression Model for Prosecution Survey

The dependent variable is whether or not someone was found guilty. The potential explanatory variables are: which court the prosecution took place at, who the prosecuting body was, what the plea was, whether the accused was present in court and whether the accused was represented in court.

The first stage of the analysis is to explore the main effects of the variables individually to establish whether we need them all in the model. The first logistic regression to be run, therefore, specifies the dichotomised guilty variable as the dependent and the five possible independent variables are entered individually.

First we consider R-squared. R-squared is a measure of how good a fit a model is. The closer R-squared is to 1, the greater the proportion of variation is being explained by the regression.

The Nagelkerke R-squared are as shown in Table 1.11. This can be interpreted as follows: 1.3 per cent of the variation in a guilty verdict can be explained by reference to the court at which the accused was prosecuted.

When all the variables were entered individually they all lead to a significant improvement in the model; they all had a significant impact on explaining the variation in the guilty verdict and therefore should all be included in the final model.

The next stage is to put all the explanatory variables into the model to establish which have the greatest impact on the guilty verdict.

One interesting and informative way of going about multiple regression is to take the analysis one step at a time. The method specified is a forward stepwise procedure in which the variables are added one at a time until no further improvements in fit can be obtained.

Table 1.11   The Nagelkerke table

Variable	Nagelkerke R-squared
Court	0.013
Who was the prosecutor	0.141
Plea	0.350
Was the accused present in court	0.174
Was the accused represented in court	0.174

For each of the variables entered, the analysis system used (SNAP) asks for specification of a reference category (either first or last category), and this provides a constant for comparison. The reference categories for each variable are shown in an example below:

Table 1.12   The variable and the reference category

Variable	Reference category
Court?	Newcastle-under-Lyme
Who is the prosecutor?	DVLA
Was the accused present in court?	Yes the accused was present in court
Was the accused represented in court?	Yes the accused was represented in court
Plea	Guilty

These reference categories are important when interpreting the model.

Interpretation of Overall Regression Model

- The odds of being found guilty for those who pleaded 'not guilty' are about 0.021 times the odds of being found guilty if you pleaded 'guilty', that is 98 per cent lower, when adjusted for the other variables.
- The odds of being found guilty for those who made no appearance are about 0.026 times the odds of being found guilty if you pleaded 'guilty', that is 74 per cent lower, when adjusted for the other variables.
- The odds of being found guilty for those prosecuted at Horseferry Road were about 4.127 times the odds of being found guilty if prosecuted at Newcastle-under-Lyme, that is 312 per cent (over three times more likely), when adjusted for the other variables.
- The odds of being found guilty for those prosecuted at Milton Keynes were about 1.51 times the odds of being found guilty if prosecuted at

Newcastle-under-Lyme, that is 50 per cent when adjusted for the other variables.

- The odds of being found guilty for those who were not represented in court are 2.107 times the odds of being found guilty for those who were represented in court, that is 210 per cent (over twice as likely), when adjusted for the other variables.

The same results can be obtained with a backward stepwise model: this starts with a full model, dropping variables one at a time.

From our model we are then able to calculate the odds of all combinations of variables: for example what are the odds of being found guilty if prosecuted by the Vehicle Inspectorate with a 'not guilty' plea entered?

Bearing in mind that in the example used earlier our reference category for plea is 'guilty' and for prosecutor it is the 'DVLA' we could construct the odds table below.

Table 1.13   Calculating the impact of the variables

	Guilty	Not guilty	No appearance	Not known
DT/DVLA	1	0.021	0.260	0.036
Vehicle Inspectorate	0.242	0.005082	0.063	0.0087
TVLEO	0.728	0.0153	0.189	0.0262
Environment Agency	0.641	0.01346	0.166	0.0230
Electricity	0.123	0.002583	0.032	0.00443

Interactions

The above model is based on the assumption that the explanatory variables are independent of each other, although in some respects this may not be the case; there may be interaction between the variables. Is it more likely that some people will plead guilty if they are prosecuted by a particular prosecuting body? Is there a relationship between plea and whether they were present in court? Is there a relationship between being represented and being present in court? If the answer to such questions is 'yes' then we must consider interactions between variables.

Given the relatively small number of explanatory variables that we have got it is possible to enter all interactions into the model and again perform a stepwise regression. Before doing this it is wise to study the cross tabulation between some of the variables – particularly those that are split into a large number of categories. Notably when we examine the cross-tabulation for plea against who the prosecutor was we will notice that some cells are in fact empty – this would detract from the robustness of the model. Therefore at this stage I removed the following prosecuting bodies from the model: British Waterways, BT Security, Electricity, HSE, Cab Law Enforcement, Department of Health and the Ministry of Agriculture (as they all had fewer than 20 cases).

Of all the interactions entered into the model, only two were found to be significant: the interaction between plea and who the prosecutor was and the interaction between plea and whether the accused was present in court.

Chapter Two

The Nature and Development of the Private Prosecution

There are over two million prosecutions every year in England and Wales. The majority of these are brought as the result of police files being handed over to the Crown Prosecution Service. This is the main mechanism of state prosecution. There are, though, also multifarious non-police agencies responsible for bringing prosecutions.

The importance of these non-police prosecutions is considerable. In the only major study of non-police prosecutions, for the Royal Commission on Criminal Procedure in 1978, Lidstone, Hogg and Sutcliffe (1980, p. 1) note that 'these prosecutions by persons or authorities other than the police are usually treated as peripheral to the English criminal justice system'. When those authors were invited by the Royal Commission to research this area, they noted that they were at first doubtful as to whether it was a sufficiently substantial matter to warrant research. Upon initial investigations, though, they soon found that the non-police prosecution was 'quantitatively more important than many have supposed' (ibid., p. 3).

Since that text a great deal has changed in the scenery of the criminal justice system. Most notably, prosecutions previously brought by the police are now brought by the Crown Prosecution Service which, following the Crown Prosecution Act 1985 came into existence in 1986. As in 1980, though, the extent of prosecutions following from non-police investigations is kept significantly lower than it might otherwise be by virtue of a policy among many agencies to use cautions, warnings and notices of various sorts for many offenders rather than resort to prosecution.

Before turning to look at the earlier research and its findings, it is appropriate to examine some general matters pertinent to the present study. Anyone analysing data related to the prosecution process, and evaluating certain sorts of case being taken through the criminal courts should seek to set that in the context of the nature and purposes of the criminal law. I do that at the outset of this study. Thereafter, I set out briefly to recount the nature and purposes of the non-CPS prosecution.

The Criminal Law

The limited aim of this excursus into criminal jurisprudence is to establish what are the popularly acknowledged purposes of the criminal justice system. There is a rich literature which looks critically at penology and the purposes of the criminal law (for example, Thompson, 1975; Hay et al., 1975; Foucault, 1979; Cohen, 1985; Lacey, 1988; Rutherford, 1993; Garland, 1990; Norrie, 1993; Ashworth, 1995; Lacey and Wells, 1998). I am principally concerned to set out the orthodoxies of the criminal justice system. This will be the doctrine against which we can compare the success or standards of the non-CPS prosecutions.

The Nature of Criminal Law

There is a view that it is impossible to be definitive about the nature of a crime because the essence of criminality changes with historical context. As Glanville Williams has observed (1983, p. 27): '... a crime (or offence) is a legal wrong that can be followed by criminal proceedings which may result in punishment.'

A crime is anything that the state has chosen to criminalise. This analysis was also taken by Lord Atkin:

> The domain of criminal jurisprudence can only be ascertained by examining what acts at any particular period are declared by the State to be crimes, and the only common nature they will be found to possess is that they are prohibited by the State and that those who commit them are punished (*Proprietary Articles Trade Association v. Att-Gen. for Canada* [1931] AC at 324).

In an attempt to escape from the circularity of these definitions of crime, some writers have sought to explain its nature in terms of the seriousness of the conduct it prohibits. Thus Williams eventually concedes (1983, p. 29) that:

> a crime is an act that is condemned sufficiently strongly to have induced the authorities (legislature or judges) to declare it to be punishable before the ordinary courts.

This is a little more helpful but it still leaves unanswered the question – 'condemned sufficiently strongly' by whom? The principle appears to owe much to the thinking of Durkheim, who remarked on the way that collective social consciousness can be enhanced by the condemnation and punishment of deviance. Criminal law therefore arguably both arises from and then bolsters social solidarity:

> It is this solidarity that repressive law expresses at least in regard to what is vital to it. Indeed, the acts which such law forbids and stigmatises as crimes are of two kinds: either they manifest directly a too violent dissimilarity between the one who commits them and the collective type; or they offend the organ of the common consciousness. In both cases the force shocked by the crime and that rejects it is thus the same. It is a result of the most vital social similarities and thus its effect is to maintain the social cohesion that arises from these similarities (1984 [1893], p. 61).

The significant point about this view of the criminal law is that it is so widely shared by those who write about and operate the criminal justice system (Lacey, 1988; Taylor, 1993), even if some of them are unaware of the subtler point made by Durkheim that the solidarity of modern societies no longer can or should be based on the repressive sanctioning of threats to common values (Nelken, 1990, p. 831). There are many variants on this outlook – some writers, for instance, do not share Durkheim's analysis of the criminal law as necessarily enhancing social solidarity – but the perception of this law as concerning serious wrongs whose commission has a deleterious effect on society is ubiquitous.

In the leading theoretical text *Criminal Law*, Smith and Hogan acknowledge the view of Sir Carleton Allen (1992, p. 16), who writes:

> Crime is crime because it consists in wrongdoing which directly and in serious degree threatens the security or well-being of society, and because it is not safe to leave it redressable only by compensation of the party injured.

The public nature of crimes is evidenced by the fact that technically, any citizen is permitted to bring a prosecution after a crime, he or she does not have to establish a personal interest or *locus standi* as in civil proceedings (although there is provision in s.24 of the Prosecution of Offences Act, 1985 for the High Court, on the application of the Attorney-General, to restrain a vexatious prosecutor).

If a citizen begins a prosecution, he or she may not discontinue it at will because it is not only his concern but that of all citizens (*R v. Wood* (1832) B & Ad 657). If a prosecution succeeds and sentence is passed, a pardon cannot be granted by the instigator of the prosecution, it can only be granted by the Crown.

In an earlier edition of their text, Smith and Hogan reported (1988, p. 12) with approval the view of Edmund Davies J. as he then was, in 1963, speaking about the 'prime object of the criminal law' as being the 'protection of the public and the maintenance of law and order'. Addressing the Magistrates' Association he said: 'It seems to me that ... every court sentence should primarily be surveyed in the light of one test: is that the best thing to do in the interest of the community?'

A similar outlook can be found in the writings of early and modern jurisprudence and in may historical accounts. The *raison d'etre* of criminal law is seen as the provision of basic protection of social interests. In his *Commentaries on The Laws of England*, William Blackstone contended (1979 [1769], p. 5) that the distinction between private wrongs and crimes was:

> that private wrongs, or civil injuries, are an infringement or privation of the civil rights which belong to individuals, considered merely as individuals; public wrongs or crimes and misdemeanours are a breach and violation of the public rights and duties, *due to the whole community, in its social aggregate capacity.* As if I detain a field from another man, to which the law has given him a right, this is a civil injury, and not a crime; for here only the right of an individual is concerned, and it is immaterial to the public, which of us is in possession of the land: but treason, murder and robbery are properly marked among crimes; since besides the injury done to individuals, they strike at the very being of society... [emphasis added].

Bentham presents a very similar view. Under the heading 'Reasons for Erecting Certain Acts into Offences', he writes in *The Theory of Legislation* that the criterion of whether conduct should be made a criminal offence should be 'utility' rather than the inherited prejudices of custom. Conduct is to be weighed, he suggests, so as to determine whether the good that results from it is outweighed by the bad; a task facilitated by the distinction between evils of the first, second, and third orders (1975, p. 33):

> Am I to examine an act which attacks the security of an individual? I compare all the Pleasure, or, in other words, all the profit, which results to the author of the act, with all the evil, or all the loss, which results to the party injured. I see at once that the evil of the first order surpasses the good of the first order. But I do not stop there. The action under consideration produces throughout society danger and alarm. The evil which at first was only individual spreads everywhere, under the form of fear. The pleasure resulting from the action belongs solely to the actor; the pain reaches a thousand – ten thousand – all. This disproportion, already prodigious, appears infinite upon passing to the evil of the third order,

and considering that, if the act in question is not suppressed, there will result from it ... the dissolution of society.

The jurisprudence of H.L.A. Hart is distinguishable from that of Blackstone in several important areas but they share a very similar premise relating to the nature of the criminal law. Hart has argued that a legal system arises from a combination of primary and secondary rules. Primary rules concern rudimentary social obligations and impose duties; the rules here relate to the basic needs of society and their aim is to ensure survival: '... for our concern is with social arrangements for continued existence not with those of a suicide club' (1961, p. 188).

The secondary rules confer public and private powers regulating the application of primary rules. Criminal law occupies an important place within the province of primary rules. Writing about the 'minimum content of natural law', Hart suggests that, given survival as an aim, law and morals must include a minimum specific content. He bases this contention on 'five simple truisms' (1961, pp. 189–95). Calling a proposition a 'truism' discounts any need to adduce argument or evidence to corroborate or verify it and consequently, Hart's propositions are left unsupported by any appropriate anthropological, economic or historical evidence, and, it is respectfully suggested are highly contentious and questionable. Such argument, though, is outside the purview of this discussion. It is in these 'truisms' however that we find Hart's justification for the criminal law. Hart's first point is that because of our 'human vulnerability' we need rules to restrict the use of violence. We are 'both occasionally prone to, and normally vulnerable to, bodily attack'. Second, we have 'approximate equality' so we need a system of mutual forbearance and compromise. This makes life 'less nasty, less brutish and less short than unrestrained aggression for beings thus approximately equal'. Third, we are all beings of 'limited altruism', neither devils nor angels; this, it is contended, makes a system of mutual forbearance both possible and necessary. Fourth, we suffer scarce and 'limited resources', so property law, it is argued, is necessary to lend order to the process. This essentially political judgement is presented as axiomatic. Fifth, as we have 'limited understanding and strength of will' we need law to deal with those who do not recognise the value of the rules of forbearance: 'All are tempted at times to prefer their own immediate interests and, in the absence of special organisation for their detection and punishment, many would succumb to the temptation' (1961, p. 193).

Although, as Field and Jorg have commented (1991, p. 159) Hart's notion of moral responsibility is founded upon capacities to differentiate right from wrong and to act accordingly, his ultimate justification for criminal law rests on the less metaphysical dictates of social survival and welfare.

Again, this approach is reflected in many legal-historical accounts. Kiralfy (1958, p. 153) states that the essential object of criminal law is 'the preservation of order in the community, and only indirectly the punishment of any injury that may be done to any individual'.

If there is such clear consensus among those who have influenced the operation of the criminal justice system then it is reasonable to judge the success of the system's functioning: i) by the extent to which it achieves the aims expressed by the consensus view of theoreticians and practitioners; and ii) by whether it policies have been formulated in accordance with its generally accepted purposes.

The Origins of Criminal Law

There can be little doubt about the importance of the criminal law as a social institution. As the Criminal Law Commissioners noted in 1843:

> The high and paramount importance of the Criminal Law consists in this consideration, that upon its due operation the enforcement of every other branch of the law ... depends. [And] there is [no branch] which is so capable of being made intelligible to all classes of persons, or which, in its relations and bearings, is calculated to excite greater attention and interest – none, the knowledge of which can tend more effectually to convince all ranks of Your Majesty's subjects that the laws are founded on just principles, having regard to the protection of all, and equally binding on all, and consequently to impress the duty and induce the habit of prompt obedience (Seventh Report, p. 4, quoted in Norrie, 1993, p. 17).

This aspect of the criminal law's importance has not diminished over the last 150 years. As Nelken notes (1987, p. 112), it retains a crucial ideological significance as being *the* form of law in closest touch with the public, and something which reinforces their belief in the need for 'law'.

There are differing explanations accounting for the rise of criminal law as a distinct entity. Some writers have regarded the process as being a rather anarchic development. Harding, for example, looking at nineteenth-century changes, states (1966, p. 361) that it was manufactured piecemeal by statutes 'listing offences with minute particularity which had long ago obscured any general principles'.

The legal histories are generally chronologies which chart legal developments almost entirely without reference to any social or historical factors precipitating the technical changes. The reasoning is often starkly teleological. Holdsworth, for example, notes that (1936, Vol. 11, p. 43):

> as soon as society begins to become more settled some method must be found of stopping the interminable feuds to which an unrestrained recourse to physical force obviously leads ...

This passage in Holdsworth is supposed to bridge the gap between the account of the rules relating to blood feud, and the author's discussion of *bot and wer* and the systems of compensation from which primitive criminal law emerged. Why these changes took place are left out of account except for the *petitio principii* explanation that the important changes occurred 'as soon as society became more settled'.

Similarly, Milsom locates the point of significant historical change – the genesis of a prototype criminal law recognisable as such to a modern observer – in a procedural issue which he treats as independent of its political and economic context. Thus (1981, p. 403):

> When Glanville distinguished criminal pleas from civil, his civil pleas were the real and the old personal actions; and criminal pleas were those concerning wrongs. Wrongs were not divided into two conceptual categories, offences against society to be punished, and injuries to victims who must be compensated. But they might be bought to justice at the instances of either authority or the victim, *and it is from these different procedures that the conceptual distinction grew* [emphasis added].

Again, this is historiographically problematic. A diligent and credulous reader of this sort of account would be left with the impression that criminal law arose almost as the result of procedural fortuity. Milsom moves on (ibid.) to suggest that the ancestor of the modern criminal law is found in those wrongs which were matters for royal justice, in pleas of the crown; that is 'the mechanism by which pleas of the crown were brought to justice at the instance of the crown'.

History such as this, which seeks to explain legal, governmental changes of enormous import by reference to the unfolding logic of existing legal mechanism, is of very limited value. It may be helpful for lawyers to be aware of these developments, but it is of little use beyond that. A knowledge, botanically, of how a flower blossoms, i.e. what physically in the plant causes its petals to open, will not be very useful to an enthusiast who knows nothing about flower beds, earth, seasonal weather changes or climate.

Marx and Engels, by contrast, regarded the criminal law as a code which generally sought to maintain the social and economic structure and thus could he seen as protecting the long-term economic interests of the ruling class. Unlike Hart's conception of humanity (1961, pp. 189–95) which presupposes that there must always be scarcity and limited understanding, thus warranting the protection of the criminal law; the materialist view accounts historically for the emergence of ordered criminal law, and regards the 'antisocial' element in some people as a product of their historical environment. Thus Marx and Engels argue (1970 [1845], p. 32) that:

> The history of right shows that in the earliest, most primitive epochs these individual, factual relations in their crudest form directly constituted right. With the development of civil society, hence with the development of private interests into class interests, the relations of right underwent changes and acquired a civilised form. They were no longer regarded as individual but as universal relations. At the same time, division of labour placed the protection of the conflicting interests of separate individuals into the hands of a few persons, whereby the barbaric enforcement of right also disappeared.

Moving to the extension of the criminal law, Engels (1969 [1845], p. 159) contended that, under pressure in the political economy, people become offenders 'as certainly as water abandons the fluid for the vaporous state at 80 degrees, Reaumur'.

Some modem writers have taken up this analysis and used it to interpret particular legal developments. Hall (1952), for example has argued that legal principles of theft were evolved and refined to cater for the needs of the ascendant mercantile class, led by Edward IV, who himself had a vested interest in such developments.

There was little, though, by way of an attempt to theorise within the school of historical materialism about the origins of criminal law until Pashukanis developed the application of the materialist conception of history to criminal law (1978, 1924). He argued that whereas the form of law in general emerged in line with the requirements of commodity exchange, so that contract law could he seen as the 'reflex' of economic relations, criminal law is an extension of forms generated by relationships between commodity owners. The origin of criminal law is associated with blood vengeance. At first these were not simply based on the principle of equivalent requital, *jus talionis,* but were part of an unending inter-clan fight. Vengeance first begins to be regulated by custom and becomes transformed into equivalent retribution at the time when, apart from revenge, the system of compositions or of expiatory payment is adopted; thus Pashukanis argues that the idea of the equivalent itself originates in the commodity form: felony can be seen as a particular variant of circulation, in which the exchange relation, that is the contractual relation, is determined retrospectively, after an arbitrary action by one of the parties (Pashukanis, 1978 [1924], pp. 168–9).

Public penalties were advantageous to the state in two respects. First, fiscally, and Pashukanis (p. 171) quotes Henry Maine:

> The State did not take from the defendant a composition for any wrong supposed to be done to itself, but claimed a share in the compensation awarded to the plaintiff, simply as the fair price of its time and trouble.

Apart from the benefits of augmented power that were given to the King by the geographical expansion of the 'King's Peace' through the twelfth century, it was also a very useful source of revenue – 'the fiscal profits of punishment' (Baker, 1971, p. 275).

Second, organised punishment was a means of maintaining discipline and protecting the authority of sacerdotal and military power. Diamond notes (1971, pp. 243–4) that in such changing society was to be found 'the great historical watershed'. As:

> ... it is here that Sir Henry Maine and Paul Vinogradoff located the passage from status to contract, from the kinship to the territorial principle, from extended familial controls to public law. One need not be concerned with the important distinctions among archaic societies ... for our understanding of the law. The significant point is that they are transitional. Particularly in their early phase they are the agencies that transmute customary forms of order into legal sanction.

The church's influence over early criminal law is illustrated by the fact that although sentences still retained the character of a retribution or an equivalent, the retribution ceased to be directly linked to the loss of the victim based on his claim but acquired a higher abstract significance as a divine punishment. In this way the church attempted to associate the ideological motive of atonement (*expiatio*) with the material aspect of compensation for the injury, and thus to construct, from penal law based on the principle of private revenge, a more effective means of maintaining public discipline (Pashukanis, 1978 [1924], p. 172).

Examining the development mindful of who stood to gain (or lose) what from particular changes can assist in understanding those changes. The notion of crime as a type of wrong associated with 'wickedness' or 'evil' was fostered by the early church and its doctrine of atonement by penance. It was under the Norman rule that the judgement of transgressors against the King's Peace belonged to royal justice. The degree of royal control, however, was very limited because the initiative for bringing criminals to justice still lay with the victim and his/her kin. The suit against the felon, the 'appeal of felony' was expensive and deterred many victims from taking action. Also, its principal object was retribution – the felon's property was forfeited, his chattels to the King and his lands to his feudal Lord so there was no gain for the victim. As an indication of how jealously guarded were these royal bonuses, appeals could be compounded by the victim for money but it was an offence to do so without royal permission. It was also made an offence to settle privately before bringing an appeal 'compounding a felony'. It was the imperfections of the appeal procedure and the consequent loss to the revenue when claimants started to disregard the felony and sue in trespass, that brought about the introduction, in the twelfth century (Radzinowicz, 1948), of a criminal process at the suit of the Crown.

Although similar in some respects to that of Pashukanis, a subtler and more historically sensitive approach has been advanced by Norrie. He has contended that 'the criminal law is neither rational nor principled', and criticised traditional legal scholarship, according to which (1993, p. 9) the principles upon which the criminal law is founded are natural and unhistoric in the sense that they are never seen as the product of a particular kind of society generating particular forms of social control peculiar to itself.

Norrie contends that in order to properly understand the origins and development of criminal law, its contradictions and anomalies, we must appreciate that its principles are 'historic and relative' (ibid.) rather than natural and general; that these principles were established in 'the crucible of social and political conflict' and bear the stamp of history in the contradictory ways in which they are formulated.

The Private Prosecution

As Stafford has observed (1989, p. 181) in general, anyone can bring a prosecution. Historically, this has been an important right. In *Gouriet v. Union of Post Office Workers*, Lord Wilberforce said:

The individual ... who wishes to see the law enforced has a remedy of his own: he can bring a private prosecution. This historical right which goes back to the earliest days of our legal system ... remains a valuable constitutional right against inertia or partiality on the part of authority.

Similarly, Lord Diplock, in the same case, states that:

... the need for prosecutions to be undertaken (and paid for) by private individuals has largely disappeared; but it still exists and it is a useful constitutional safeguard against capricious, corrupt or biased failure or refusal of those authorities to prosecute offenders against the criminal law.

Speaking in a parliamentary debate on the Prosecution of Offences Bill in 1984, Lord Simon of Glaisdale spoke of the foundational principle of the right to private prosecution as a 'fundamental constitutional principle of individual liberty based on the rule of law'. Addressing clause 6 of the Bill which dealt with the preservation of the right of private prosecution, Lord Simon said (Hansard (HL), 29 November 1984, Vol. 457, col. 1050):

The right of private prosecution is an important element in the rule of law. Every citizen should be able to say: 'You, the authorities of bureaucracy, the Ministers, may say that there are social or political grounds whereby one should not prosecute. I, who claim to live under the rule of law, proclaim my right to set the law in motion.' I think that this Bill is entirely right to preserve that important personal liberty.

In the earliest stages of English legal history, all prosecutions were private prosecutions called appeals of felony. The appeal of murder gave the relatives of the murdered man a chance to get something from the murderer by the threat to bring an appeal. There is evidence that the threat to bring an appeal was used to acquire compensation. Thus in 1770, the widow of John Bigby brought an appeal against his murderers, Matthew and Patrick Kennedy, which was compromised for a payment of £350. Such settlements, known as 'compounding a felony' eventually became illegal as the state developed an interest in prosecuting major cases. There were, however, financial incentives for the state to act where fines could be imposed on criminals, and there was also the expansion of the principle of the 'Kings Peace' and the governmental control of public order.

The principle that, subject to exceptions, anyone can bring a private prosecution is preserved by s.6 (1) of the Prosecution of Offences Act 1985, which states:

> ... nothing in this Part shall preclude any person from instituting criminal proceedings or conducting any criminal proceedings to which the Director's [DPP] duty to take over the conduct of proceedings does not apply.

There are, however, two main types of limitation on this 'right'. The first concerns resources and the second concerns legal powers. First, it may be of little avail to an individual that he can bring a prosecution if he does not have the resources to conduct an investigation or to bring the case. Legal aid is not available for such prosecutions. It is also relevant here that the right to bring a prosecution is not always supported with rights to investigate and garner evidence. Second, only those with legal personality can prosecute, i.e. individuals or incorporated companies. In difficult or socially problematic cases, the Director of Public Prosecutions may institute his own proceedings or take over and then drop proceedings taken out by an individual.

If there is an exception to the general rule that anyone can bring a prosecution, then this will be mentioned in the legislation that creates the offence. Stafford cites five main areas of exception to this rule (1989, pp. 183–6).

The first exception concerns legislation in which the right to prosecute is reserved to particular people. For example, s.83(1) of the Weights and Measures Act 1985 provides that:

> ... proceedings for any offence under this Act, or any instrument made under this Act, other than for proceedings for an offence under section 64, shall not be instituted except by or on behalf of a local weights and measures authority or the Chief Officer of Police for a police area.

There are also Acts which reserve the power to prosecute primarily to named bodies while also permitting a law officer of the Crown to institute proceedings in certain specified circumstances.

The second exception to the general rule that anyone can prosecute is one that arises where legislation confers a right on a named body to prosecute and requires the consent of a specified person if the right is to be accorded to someone other that the particular body. An example can be found in s.298 of the Public Health Act 1936 which states:

> Proceedings in respect of an offence created by or under the Act shall not, without the written consent of the Attorney-General, be taken by any person other than a party aggrieved, or a council or body whose function is to enforce the provisions or by laws in question, or by whom or by whose predecessors the by-law in question was made.

A third exception to the proposition that anyone can bring a prosecution concerns offences where any prosecution requires the leave of the court. For instance, when a winding-up order has been made or a provisional liquidator appointed no action or proceedings shall be proceeded with against a company except by leave of the court and subject to such terms as the court may impose.

The fourth exception concerns legislation which requires notice to be given to a specified body before a prosecution can be brought. For example, s.130(1) of the Fair Trading Act provides that where a local weights and measures authority wishes to bring certain proceedings it must notify the Director about the intended proceedings and provide a summary of the facts on which the charges are founded.

The fifth exception to the rule that anyone can bring a prosecution concerns the court's capacity to restrict vexatious litigants in order to prevent an abuse of the right. Under s.42 of the Supreme Court Act 1981, the High Court can declare someone a vexatious litigant if he or she has habitually and persistently instituted civil proceedings without reasonable grounds.

People declared as vexatious litigants have often been litigants in person but it is equally possible for someone who has taken legal advice before suing for the umpteenth time to be barred from using the courts again. The actions of a vexatious litigant are usually against a variety of people while originating from the same incident.

The Law Commission (1998) has recommended that rules requiring people to receive official permission prior to prosecuting should, in all but a few cases, be abolished. At present only a handful of private prosecutions for crimes are mounted a year after the CPS has declined to bring proceedings. In most cases, it then steps in, either to carry on the proceedings or to stop them. One high-profile case was that started unsuccessfully after the death of Stephen Lawrence. In 1995 the first private prosecution was brought, successfully, for rape – with the backing of the English Collective of Prostitutes.

In 1980, research for the Royal Commission on Criminal Procedure (Lidstone et al., 1980, p. 23) found that only 2.4 per cent of all non-police prosecutions were by private individuals. The Law Commission argues that the right, widely regarded as fundamental and a safeguard against any arbitrary refusal of the authorities to prosecute, is not exercised because of a number of obstacles. Rules requiring the prospective prosecutor to obtain official consent to proceed with the case are one hurdle; cost is another as legal aid is not available.

The present system contains many anomalies. The DPP's consent is needed, for instance, to prosecute a victim's spouse for stealing or damaging property, but is not needed to prosecute the same spouse for obtaining property by deception, wounding, blackmail, rape or attempted murder. Nor is there any logic as to why sometimes the DPP's consent is required and sometimes the consent of law officers (Law Commission, 1998, Appendix A, pp. 83–95).

The Law Commission argues that the right to bring a private prosecution should only be circumscribed in certain specified circumstances. It proposes that these are where a defendant could reasonably contend that a prosecution might violate his human rights; where an offence involves national security or international obligations; or where the offences create a high risk that the right of private prosecution will be abused and that proceedings would cause the defendant irreparable harm. The Law Commission recommends that in all other cases, the requirement to obtain consent should be abolished (Law Commission, 1998, pp. 79–83).

The Royal Commission study (Lidstone et al., 1980) had terms of reference which required it to study and make recommendations on the process of the pre-trial criminal procedure in England and Wales. It had to examine the powers and duties of the police in the investigation of crime and the way that these affect the rights of the suspect; to study the existing system for prosecuting all criminal offences; to bear in mind in doing the above, the national need to use resources efficiently and economically; and, lastly, to give regard to the proper balance between the interests of the community in seeking to bring offenders to justice and in protecting the rights and liberties of persons suspected or accused of crime. I am indebted to the work of the authors of the Royal Commission study for much of the background that I present here.

As the 1980 study shows, the great majority of cases prosecuted in the criminal courts of England and Wales are initiated by the police. The police then (before the establishment of the CPS) were responsible for the entire process of prosecution, from the initial enquiries up to and including the decision to prosecute and the conduct of the case in court (although the latter may be delegated to a lawyer acting for the police). Yet in a significant minority of cases the police were not the prosecutors, a state of affairs that still obtains today.

The prosecutor can be a personally aggrieved citizen, a business employee instructed by his head office; an inspector of the Ministry of Transport; an officer of a water authority pursuing those who use hoses to wash cars without proper arrangements to pay for the use of that water; a weights and measures inspector of a town council; or some other person who is employed in the business of regulating our conduct. Books and speeches may contain glowing references to the Englishman's 'cherished right' of private prosecution but few have enquired seriously into the extent of the use of that right and fewer still into prosecutions by government departments, local authorities and the like. The 1980 study uncovered 'a bewildering variety of offences prosecuted by a bewildering variety of prosecuting bodies, we also discovered a vast further potential for prosecution which was not being realised' (p. 2). The study also found that different prosecuting agencies had very different approaches, that their relationship with the police was very different and that at the end of the study they were 'only too well aware of having merely scratched the surface of a topic that is much more demanding of serious scholarly and administrative attention than we had ever supposed' (ibid.).

The Historical Context of the Right to a Private Prosecution

The huge rise in the level of crime arising from the rapid social and economic changes of the late eighteenth century coincided with a growing inadequacy of the magistracy as a form of administrative control and the absence of any professional police force. The main responsibility for law enforcement

> rested with the private citizen whose sense of duty must have been sadly dampened by the realisation that the costs of bringing a criminal to justice had to be met out of his own pocket (Edwards, 1964, p. 338, cited by Lidstone et al., 1980, p. 2).

After 1752, legislation making provision for payment of prosecution costs was passed, but these payments were never adequate and did little to encourage the private individual to prosecute. Prosecuting societies began to arise, and were themselves signs of the struggle to control lawlessness. By 1839 there were more than 500 prosecuting societies in existence.

Modern civil police forces were being formed in England and Wales from 1829 but none of the legislation setting up these police forces referred to any prosecutorial role for the police. When the police did start to prosecute it was in their capacity as private citizens. As the police began to prosecute more so the prosecuting societies died away. Perhaps the first call for a public prosecution was the proposal in 1534 from Henry VIII that laws:

> are not put into force unless it be by malice, rancour and evil will. Better it were that they had never been made, unless they should be put in due and perfect execution (cited in Lidstone et al., 1980, p. 2).

To remedy the imperfect execution of the law, Henry unsuccessfully proposed that Sergeants of the Common Weal act as prosecutors. Although the nineteenth century saw a number of proposals for a formal prosecuting agency none was successful. The campaign though did succeed in creating the office of the Director of Public Prosecutions first in 1879 and then on a fresh basis in 1908. These Acts though specified that nothing in them should interfere in the right of any person's institute or undertake any criminal proceedings. Succeeding legislation has however gradually eroded the general right of private prosecution by requiring the consent of the DPP or the Attorney General before a prosecution can be launched or by confining the right to prosecute to particular agencies. Thus in theory the private individual is theoretically free to prosecute anyone although this right is substantially circumscribed by different pieces of legislation.

The right of private prosecution has been characterised as 'a safety valve'; 'a very important control over executive power'; 'a fundamental principal of English criminal law'; 'an important constitutional safeguard'; and 'a valuable constitutional safeguard against inertia or partiality on the part of authority'.

The report of the Royal Commission study notes that (Lidstone et al., 1980, p. 3):

> the 20th century has seen the rise of a new kind of private prosecution, if it may be so called. The increasing complexity of an advanced industrial–urban society, and the increasing dependency of the State intervening in various aspects of economic and social life, have led to the creation of many new central and local government functions, not a few of which have involved concomitant criminal offences. For example the creation of a state social security system requires that fraudulent claims on social security be policed; the creation of the British Broadcasting Corporation financed by license fees requires that license revenue be collected and evasion punished; the increasing role of the State in consumer protection and the regulation of business requires the creation of trading standards enforced by an appropriate authority ….

The authors argue that is has usually been considered appropriate to allow the responsibility for the prosecution of offences under such legislation to fall upon a government department, the local authority or relevant agency which has general oversight of the subject matter in question. They note that it is of interest that the great majority of offences created under such legislation are nonindictable (i.e. triable only before magistrates), even though the sums of money involved in the offence may be much greater than those in many indictable offences like minor theft. They say the main reason for this would appear to be a belief that many such offences are not 'real crimes', but, rather, regulatory offences which happen to be dealt with under criminal law for the sake of convenience. The prevalence of this rather doubtful view has been brought home to us at many points in this research project; it is one among many reasons for rejecting as misplaced the view of one American observer that 'the closest condition to an official public prosecution in England and Wales are the cases brought by government departments, local authorities and certain ministries of national government' (Sigler, 1974 p. 644, cited by Lidstone et al., 1980, p. 4).

The literature on this subject that existed before the Lidstone study was very slender. There was a study from Carson (1970a), who examined the enforcement of factory legislation and showed a pattern of substantial law violation countered almost exclusively by the use of formal administrative procedures rather than the prosecution of offenders. Dickens (1970) studied local authority prosecutions and reviewed such cases under four heads – education, consumer protection, vehicle licensing and public health. This study also concludes that local authorities saw their duties as imposing upon them an obligation to achieve prescribed results and not simply to enforce the provisions of the law *per se*; thus recourse to the courts was very much seen as a last resort, but prosecutions were invariably successful – mainly because offences were of strict liability and offered no defence. A study by Cranston (1979) looked at the regulation of business activities and the prosecution of offences in a London borough, a metropolitan county and a non-metropolitan county. His conclusion that trading standards department do not see their primary purpose as being the prosecution of offences is, Lidstone notes (p. 3) in line with that reached by Dickens. Two other previous studies were those of Mawby (1978, 1979) and Hadden (1968). Mawby examined in some detail the detection methods and prosecution policy of the National Television Licence Records Office which prosecutes for licence offences. This agency had one of the largest of the police inputs into the criminal justice system. Hadden investigated the role of the Department of Trade in its task of controlling company fraud and concluded that the system of inspection served little useful purpose. A 1967 study (Zander and Glasser, 1967) found that in a study of five London courts only 1 per cent of the cases were prosecuted by private individuals. Another study conducted in Hertfordshire in 1969 produced similar results: only 81 of 9,341 prosecutions were conducted by private individuals, less than 1 per cent. Of the 81 prosecutions 22 were for common assault the remainder being for theft, mainly shopping (Wilcox, 1972, pp. 3–4).

The 1980 study encountered a terminological problem – the prosecutions being looked at by the team could not really be described as 'private prosecutions' because many of the prosecuting bodies like local authorities and the TV Licence Record Office etc. were public bodies. Lord Devlin had once used the term 'unofficial prosecution', but in the end the team adopted the phrase 'non-police prosecutions' (Devlin, 1960, p.16).

In the Royal Commission study, the Registers of 12 magistrates' courts were examined with the information for the year 1977 being extracted from each court. The researchers in this project gathered data from the court Registers for every month of 1977 in courts at Sheffield, Dover, Hereford City, and Hereford County. Data from the court records was gathered for alternate months in 1977 at courts in Cardiff, Newcastle, Lincoln City, Lincoln (Kesteven), Bow Street, Croydon, Horseferry Road and Mansion House. In the case of the six-month study the figures were adjusted accordingly. So, for example, although the number of defendants in non-police cases in six months at Newcastle was actually 741, the figure shown in the Royal Commission study (Lidstone et al., 1980) is 1482.

One of the courts in the Royal Commission study is Horseferry Road. The reason for its selection is worth noting:

> Horseferry Road Court was added at a later stage, after we had become aware of the special policy of the Metropolitan Police in encouraging private prosecutions for shoplifting offences ... Horseferry Road serves an area in the West of London containing many large stores, and was more likely than was Bow Street to show the effect of the police policy on shoplifting.

This is of interest here because, as will be seen later in the present study, the policy of the Metropolitan Police is now not to encourage private store prosecutions and there were at Horseferry Road, in fact, no such prosecutions found on the records for 1988.

The Broad Findings of The Royal Commission Court Study

Altogether, across the 12 courts, the study found 16,515 defendants who were prosecuted privately during 1997. These defendants, some of whom were prosecuted for more than one offence, were accused of a total 21,735 offences. There is some considerable difference between the volume of private prosecution work in the different courts. Thus, there were in 1977 in Sheffield

2,654 such prosecutions as against only 374 heard at Dover magistrates' court and only 20 at Lincoln (Kesteven). At Sheffield and London's Bow Street magistrates' courts private prosecutions represented 16.1 per cent and 15.4 per cent respectively of the overall number of prosecutions dealt with by those courts, whereas at Hereford City magistrates' court private prosecutions represented only 0.8 per cent of all the prosecutions brought there.

The study shows that (Lidstone et al., 1980, p. 15) almost 70 per cent of the non-police input into the 12 courts was generated by just four agencies – the Post Office, the British Transport Police, the Department of the Environment and local authorities. In the study 24.8 per cent of all defendants in the non-police cases were prosecuted by the Post Office (mainly television licence cases). The other agencies, followed here by the percentage of all defendants in non-police cases in this study that they represented) were: retail stores (9.5 per cent); DHSS (7.2 per cent); London Transport (6.2 per cent); Customs & Excise (3.1 per cent); private individuals (2.4 per cent); Regional Traffic Area (1.2 per cent); the Probation Service etc. (0.8 per cent); the Health and Safety Executive (0.4 per cent); the RSPCA (0.2 per cent); Water Authority (0.1 per cent); Inland Revenue (0.1 per cent); and the Department of Trade (0.1 per cent).

Only 2.4 per cent of the defendants in the study were prosecuted by private individuals. The majority of such prosecutions were for common assault (364 offences out of a total of 444 offences, committed by 392 defendants). The rural courts had few such prosecutions (Lidstone et al., 1980, p. 23).

The study notes (p. 25) that most agencies have primary functions which are not prosecutorial; prosecution being used only to assist in their main functions. This is particularly true in relation to revenue collecting agencies like the Post Office and the Department of the Environment. They face a large population of possible 'at risk' offenders and the offence is easy to prove so prosecution becomes an effective means of maximising revenue collection. This is not so in the case of the Inland Revenue and, to a lesser extent, Customs and Excise since offences are much more difficult to prove.

> The fact that they have powers to dispose of offences and impose penalties without recourse to prosecution, means that prosecution is a last resort and consequently not as effective a means of maximising the revenue collection. One therefore expects large numbers of prosecutions from agencies such as the Post Office and the Department of the Environment and fewer from Customs and Excise and the Inland Revenue.

Plea and Outcome

The Royal Commission study found that, with the exception of prosecutions by private individuals, there was in all instances a high rate of guilty pleas (always 88 per cent or greater). The study notes that this is not surprising given the nature of offences prosecuted (many are strict liability offences which admit of no or very limited defence); and also the fact that most agencies prosecute only as a last resort, thus eliminating many of the weaker cases before the prosecution begins. In the case of prosecutions brought by the Post Office (most of which were for TV Licence evasion) 98 per cent of all those charged pleaded guilty. Similarly in 93 per cent of cases brought by the DHSS, defendants pleaded guilty, and of those prosecuted by the Regional Traffic Commissioners (prosecutions for offences related to lorries etc.) 98 per cent of defendants pleaded guilty. The success rate of the various prosecuting agencies, judged by the percentage of contested cases (i.e. where there is a 'not guilty' plea) that each agency wins was found by the study to be highly variable. The Post Office, for example, won 77 per cent of its contested cases, whereas retail stores won only 37 per cent of theirs. British Transport Police, London Transport and the Local Authorities all only succeeded in less than 65 per cent of their contested cases. Overall, however, the conviction rate for non-police prosecutions, i.e. convictions where there has been either a not guilty or a guilty plea, is very high, excluding private individuals, who only succeeded in 61 per cent of the cases they brought, no prosecuting agency had a success rate of less than 94 per cent.

One of the key findings in the Royal Commission study (Lidstone et al., 1980, p. 29) was that for broadly equivalent offences it makes little difference to the outcome whether a prosecution is brought by the police or by a non-police prosecutor. The authors looked at a range of ordinary criminal offences prosecuted then by the police, like wounding, burglary, theft, shoplifting and criminal damage, and noted that in cases like these where the defendant pleads not guilty there is a approximately 50 per cent likelihood that he will be nevertheless convicted. This is a broadly similar rate as those for the non-police agency prosecutions in respect of cases that require specific proofs of elements like 'intent' which feature in cases of theft brought by retail stores and the deception offences prosecuted by the Transport Police. The Royal Commission study also found that over 80 per cent of offences proved by 10 of the 80 main listed main prosecutors were disposed of by a fine of £50 or less. Only in the case of prosecutions by the Health and Safety Executive, Customs and Excise and the Department of Trade were larger fines imposed to any significant extent. The extent to which parties in these private prosecutions were legally represented in the Royal Commission study is not entirely accurately recorded as the information was not always registered clearly in the court files. However, in the 12 courts taken together, prosecutors were legally represented in 52 per cent of cases, and represented by an employee of the agency in 42 per cent. There were some notable exceptions; so, for example, at Horseferry Road where prosecutions for shoplifting abounded, solicitors prosecuted in 89 per cent of cases, probably reflecting the policy of large stores to retain solicitors for these cases (Lidstone et al., 1980, p. 30). In regard to the defence, the study found that 95 per cent of defendants were not represented by a lawyer. This is largely explained by the fact that the majority of such defendants pleaded guilty and that legal aid is unavailable for the majority of offences prosecuted. In conclusion in this area, the authors note that:

> The overall picture that one derives of plea, outcome and representation in non-police cases is therefore one of agency employees or solicitors, prosecuting unrepresented defendants, who almost invariably plead guilty – but who when they do plead not guilty, are nevertheless usually found guilty – and are fined £50 or less (Lidstone et al., 1980, p. 30).

How far, if at all, have these patterns altered in the 20 years since the Royal Commission study? Has the establishment of the Crown Prosecution Service in 1985 and the extensive deregulation in some areas (like the power industries and transport) had any effect upon the behaviour of agency, departmental and private company prosecutions? In the next chapter, I turn to examine some principal findings of the court research carried out for this study.

Chapter Three

The Broad Findings of the Court Study

What follows in this chapter is an account of some of the findings from the court study. As the base consisted of 9,689 cases brought by 21 agencies across three courts the extent of possible detail in presentation here is considerable. Where data was generated but did not appear to have any possible significance for legal or social policy or managerial issues concerning agencies or the courts, it has been omitted from coverage here. Throughout the chapter reference is made to the five tables (P1 to P5) containing information about the research findings using the prosecuting agency as the variable. These tables are located in Appendix 2.

Table 3.1 shows the number of non-police prosecutions by court. They were collected from the registers for the year 1998.

Table 3.1   Prosecutions by court

Absolute analysis % respondents	Base	Missing No reply	Which court is the information from?		
			Horseferry Road	Milton Keynes	Newcastle-under-Lyme
	9,689	–	3,211	5,226	1,252
	100.0%	–	33.1%	53.9%	12.9%

Of the base – 9,689 – 80 per cent of the non-police prosecutions were brought by four agencies: *Borough/County Councils* generated 41.2 per cent (3,991 cases); *DT/DVLA* 23.9 per cent (2,320 cases); *TVLEO* 9.5 per cent (920 cases); *DSS* 5.4 per cent (527 cases).

The remaining 20 per cent of prosecutions ranked in order of number of defendants were brought by: *Vehicle Inspectorate* (535, 5.5 per cent); *London Buses* (427, 4.4 per cent); *SW Trains* (271, 2.8 per cent); *Inland Revenue* (210, 2.2 per cent); *Customs & Excise* (123, 1.3 per cent); *Education Welfare* (118, 1.2 per cent); *Environment Agency* 97, 1.0 per cent); *DTI* (37, 0.4 per cent); *Trading Standards* (33, 0.3 per cent); *RSPCA* (25, 0.3 per cent); *Electricity Supply Companies* (18, 0.2 per cent); *HSE* (15, 0.2 per cent); *British Waterways* (10, 0.1 per cent); *Cab Law Enforcement* (6, 0.1 per cent); *BT Security* (4 cases); *Dept of Health* (1 case); *Ministry of Agriculture* (1 case).

If these figures are extrapolated on to a national scale we can get some rough idea of what is taking place across the country. Such a technique is clearly not ideal but it is about the only practical way of arriving at a rough estimate of what is occurring. The number of prosecutions brought by agencies in the course of a year is not recorded at any magistrates' court nor is some form of global figure for the whole country recorded by the Home Office or Lord Chancellor's Department. The only way to compute the figure for any particular court is to do what was done in this project, i.e. for the cases to be identified and counted from the court registers for one year. This took six months of laborious effort to complete in respect of just three courts. The costs of replicating that work across all the magistrates' courts of England and Wales, of which there are some 460, would therefore be prohibitive.[1]

A great many courts have jurisdictions smaller than the smallest in this research project, and deal with considerably fewer agency prosecutions. Many other magistrates' courts, however, have much higher numbers of agency cases than those dealt with in this study. Some courts – for example, in poor districts of cities – have a much higher caseload of DSS cases (there was a total of only 527 cases here from 9,689) while also having a heavy load of vehicle and TV cases. If we take the figure of 1,000 agency cases per court per year (to err on the side of an underestimate, as even the lowest number in our study was 1,252 for 1998 in Newcastle-under-Lyme) then we arrive at an estimate of approximately 460,000 agency prosecutions a year.

I now turn to present data concerning each of the prosecuting authorities.

Borough/County Councils

By far the highest number of prosecutions (41.2 per cent) were brought by the Borough/County Councils (B/CCs). Out of a total of 3,989 prosecutions, *Milton Keynes* generated 2,115 (53 per cent), *Horseferry Road* 1,858 (46.6 per cent) and *Newcastle-under-Lyme* 16 (0.4 per cent).

Overall the greatest proportion of prosecutions were brought for offences under Road Traffic Act and related Regulations including parking offences. These accounted for 63.8 per cent (2,545) of the cases. The majority of these defendants (52.6 per cent, 2,881) were prosecuted by MKBC and Bucks CC at Milton Keynes. The relative lack of traffic prosecutions by the council at Newcastle-under-Lyme is explicable in by reference to local council policy there: traffic related matters including parking violations are left almost entirely to the police.

Other offences prosecuted at Milton Keynes included seven of selling

Table 3.2   Disposals upon conviction

Absolute analysis %
Break %
Respondents

(Each prosecutor cell shows: count / Absolute analysis % / Break %. The "Respondents" total row shows count / %.)

Who was the prosecutor?	Base / Respondents	Remanded on bail	Remanded in custody	Imprisonment	Probation	Community Service	Combination Order	Absolute discharge	Conditional discharge	Sentence suspended
Respondents	6,554	126 / 1.9%	5 / 0.1%	14 / 0.2%	22 / 0.3%	56 / 0.9%	8 / 0.1%	80 / 1.2%	95 / 1.4	2 / 0.0%
DT/DVLA	1,853 / 28.3%	15 / 0.8% / 11.9%	0.0% / 0.0%	1 / 0.1% / 7.1%	0.0% / 0.0%	0.0% / 0.0%	0.0% / 0.0%	21 / 1.1% / 26.3%	2 / 0.1% / 2.1%	0.0% / 0.0%
Vehicle Inspectorate	360 / 5.5%	3 / 0.8% / 2.4%	0.0% / 0.0%	0.0% / 0.0%	0.0% / 0.0%	0.0% / 0.0%	0.0% / 0.0%	14 / 3.9% / 17.5%	0.0% / 0.0%	0.0% / 0.0%
TVLEO	654 / 10.0%	6 / 0.9% / 4.8%	0.0% / 0.0%	0.0% / 0.0%	0.0% / 0.0%	0.0% / 0.0%	0.0% / 0.0%	2 / 0.3% / 2.5%	3 / 0.5% / 3.2%	0.0% / 0.0%
Environmental Agency	72 / 1.1%	2 / 2.8% / 1.6%	0.0% / 0.0%	0.0% / 0.0%	1 / 1.4% / 4.5%	0.0% / 0.0%	0.0% / 0.0%	0.0% / 0.0%	0.0% / 0.0%	0.0% / 0.0%
Electricity	5 / 0.1%	5 / 100.0% / 4.0%	0.0% / 0.0%	0.0% / 0.0%	0.0% / 0.0%	0.0% / 0.0%	0.0% / 0.0%	0.0% / 0.0%	0.0% / 0.0%	0.0% / 0.0%
DSS	217 / 3.3%	69 / 31.8% / 54.8%	5 / 2.3% / 100.0%	9 / 4.1% / 64.3%	14 / 6.5% / 63.6%	52 / 24.0% / 92.9%	8 / 3.7% / 100.0%	0.0% / 0.0%	27 / 12.4% / 28.4%	1 / 0.5% / 50.0%
RSPCA	7 / 0.1%	0.0% / 0.0%	0.0% / 0.0%	1 / 14.3% / 7.1%	0.0% / 0.0%	0.0% / 0.0%	0.0% / 0.0%	0.0% / 0.0%	0.0% / 0.0%	0.0% / 0.0%
DTI	5 / 0.1%	0.0% / 0.0%	0.0% / 0.0%	0.0% / 0.0%	0.0% / 0.0%	1 / 20.0% / 1.6%	0.0% / 0.0%	0.0% / 0.0%	2 / 40.0% / 2.1%	1 / 20.0% / 50.0%

	C1	C2	C3	C4	C5	C6	C7	C8	C9	C10
Trading Standards	18 / 0.3%	7 / 38.9% / 5.6%	0.0% / 0.0%	0.0% / 0.0%	0.0% / 0.0%	0.0% / 0.0%	0.0% / 0.0%	0.0% / 0.0%	4 / 22.2% / 4.2%	0.0% / 0.0%
Education Welfare	77 / 1.2%	5 / 6.5% / 4.0%	0.0% / 0.0%	0.0% / 0.0%	7 / 9.1% / 31.0%	0.0% / 0.0%	0.0% / 0.0%	3 / 3.9% / 3.8%	28 / 33.8% / 27.4%	0.0% / 0.0%
British Waterways	9 / 0.1%	0.0% / 0.0%	0.0% / 0.0%	0.0% / 0.0%	0.0% / 0.0%	0.0% / 0.0%	0.0% / 0.0%	0.0% / 0.0%	0.0% / 0.0%	0.0% / 0.0%
BT Security	3 / 0.0%	1 / 33.3% / 0.0%	0.0% / 0.0%	0.0% / 0.0%	0.0% / 0.0%	0.0% / 0.0%	0.0% / 0.0%	0.0% / 0.0%	1 / 33.3% / 0.0%	0.0% / 0.0%
Inland Revenue	2 / 0.0%	0.0% / 0.0%	0.0% / 0.0%	0.0% / 0.0%	0.0% / 0.0%	0.0% / 0.0%	0.0% / 0.0%	0.0% / 0.0%	0.0% / 0.0%	0.0% / 0.0%
Customs and Excise	15 / 0.2%	1 / 6.7% / 0.8%	0.0% / 0.0%	2 / 13.3% / 14.3%	0.0% / 0.0%	1 / 6.7% / 1.8%	0.0% / 0.0%	0.0% / 0.0%	2 / 13.3% / 2.1%	0.0% / 0.0%
HSE	7 / 0.1%	1 / 14.3% / 0.8%	0.0% / 0.0%	0.0% / 0.0%	0.0% / 0.0%	0.0% / 0.0%	0.0% / 0.0%	0.0% / 0.0%	0.0% / 0.0%	0.0% / 0.0%
SW Trains	189 / 2.9%	0.0% / 0.0%	0.0% / 0.0%	0.0% / 0.0%	0.0% / 0.0%	0.0% / 0.0%	0.0% / 0.0%	0.0% / 0.0%	2 / 1.1% / 2.1%	0.0% / 0.0%
Cab Law Enforcement	5 / 0.1%	0.0% / 0.0%	0.0% / 0.0%	0.0% / 0.0%	0.0% / 0.0%	0.0% / 0.0%	0.0% / 0.0%	0.0% / 0.0%	0.0% / 0.0%	0.0% / 0.0%
London Buses	299 / 4.6%	0.0% / 0.0%	0.0% / 0.0%	0.0% / 0.0%	0.0% / 0.0%	0.0% / 0.0%	0.0% / 0.0%	5 / 1.7% / 6.3%	2 / 0.7% / 2.1%	0.0% / 0.0%
Department of Health	0.0% / 0.0%	0.0% / 0.0%	0.0% / 0.0%	0.0% / 0.0%	0.0% / 0.0%	0.0% / 0.0%	0.0% / 0.0%	0.0% / 0.0%	0.0% / 0.0%	0.0% / 0.0%
Borough/County Councils	2,757 / 42.1%	11 / 0.4% / 8.7%	0.0% / 0.0%	1 / 0.0% / 7.1%	0.0% / 0.0%	2 / 0.1% / 3.6%	0.0% / 0.0%	35 / 1.3% / 43.8%	24 / 0.9% / 25.3%	0.0% / 0.0%
Ministry of Agriculture	0.0% / 0.0%	0.0% / 0.0%	0.0% / 0.0%	0.0% / 0.0%	0.0% / 0.0%	0.0% / 0.0%	0.0% / 0.0%	0.0% / 0.0%	0.0% / 0.0%	0.0% / 0.0%

bone in beef; six for offences under Food Safety Act and related Regulations; one of supplying a video with no classification certification; eight of offering goods for sale contrary to Trade Marks Act 1994; and two of transmitting noise amounting to a statutory nuisance.

At Horseferry Road the majority of prosecutions – 1,087 (58.5 per cent) – were brought for having no street trading licence. In addition, 463 (11.6 per cent) defendants were prosecuted for offences under Road Traffic Act and related Regulations; 91 (4.9 per cent) for displaying a card in a telephone kiosk and 46 (2.5 per cent) for supplying a video with no class certification. There were also 32 prosecutions for offences under Food Safety Act and related Regulations; 29 for using premises without or not in accordance with a licence; 17 for displaying an advertisement without consent; 17 for offering goods for sale contrary to Trade Marks Act 1994; eight for accepting payment contrary to Accommodation Agencies Act 1953; seven for transmitting noise amounting to a statutory nuisance; seven for employing an unregistered door supervisor; six for wilfully obstructing free passage along a highway; six for retaining a skip or scaffolding on highway without permission; six for selling food unfit for human consumption; five for placing a product on the market without permission; five for committing surgery under anaesthesia in an unregistered clinic; four for offences under the Clean Air Act 1993; four for carrying on work outside specified hours; three for selling food not of the nature demanded; three for not declaring an interest in premises; three for supplying fireworks to a person under 18; three for offering goods for sale contrary to Trade Descriptions Act; two for failing to display a corporate name; two for misleading customers as to price; and one for failing to state a business name on a fax.

Newcastle-under-Lyme Magistrates Court had the least number of prosecutions by borough and county councils. Six defendants were prosecuted for offences under the Environment Protection Act 1990; three for offences under Food Safety Act/Regulations; two for offences under the Clean Air Act, and one for each of breach of planning control, breach of Road Traffic Act/ Regulations, failing to remove and dispose of dog faeces, abandoning rubbish, and failing to notify the Council of change of address and circumstances.

Pleas Of the 3,991 cases prosecuted by B/CCs 759, (13.8 per cent) defendants pleaded guilty and 161 (4.1 per cent) not guilty. In the majority of cases – 2,221 (55.7 per cent) – no appearance was recorded and there were 645 (16.2 per cent) not known (P1).

Verdicts Two thousand seven hundred and fify seven (69.1 per cent) of the defendants were found guilty and 4 (0.1 per cent) not guilty. Eleven were remanded on bail and four remanded in custody. Five hundred and sixty-one (14.1 per cent) cases were adjourned, 447 (11.2 per cent) withdrawn/dismissed, eight warrants issued and 198 (5.0 per cent) summons not served (P2).

Disposal Of the 2,757 defendants convicted only one was imprisoned. The vast majority – 2,684 (97.4 per cent) – were given a fine, 11 (0.4 per cent) were remanded on bail and two (0.1 per cent) given a Community Service Order. In 35 (1.3 per cent) cases there was an absolute discharge and in 24 (0.9 per cent) a conditional discharge (P3).

Presence in court and representation Only 105 (2.6 per cent) of defendants were recorded as being present in court; 2,628 (65.8 per cent) were recorded not present, with 1,076 (27.0 per cent) not known (P4). Seventeen (0.4 per cent) accused were represented, 365 (9.1 per cent) not represented and 3,424 (85.8 per cent) not known (P5).

Several points here are worthy of particular comment. First, it is clear that a remarkable range of offences is being prosecuted under the auspices of the council. In effect this means that a great deal of the different behaviours that society and the legal system label as 'criminal' (in the sense that they are prosecutable in the criminal courts and can be sanctioned accordingly) are being investigated and prosecuted by agencies other than the police and the Crown Prosecution Service. However, even though these matters are being taken through the criminal justice system, the evidence here suggests that they are not seen by defendants as particularly important or consequential events: of the 3,991 cases, only 105 (2.6 per cent) of the defendants were recorded as being in court for the case. Although the rate of conviction in this category is the same as for the outcome of magistrates' court prosecutions in general, i.e. 70 per cent,[2] only one of the 2,757 convicted defendants was given a fine, whereas looking at the caseload of magistrates' courts in general, 10 per cent of those found guilty were given an immediate custodial sentence.[3]

DT/DVLA

Of the 2,320 cases (23.9 per cent) prosecuted by the DT/DVLA, the vast majority – 80.3 per cent (1,862) – were prosecuted at Milton Keynes. Most of these (1,851, 99.4 per cent) were under the Vehicle Excise Registration Act 1994 and Road Vehicles (Registration and Licensing) Regulations 1971 for

Table 3.3   DT/DVLA prosecutions and the courts

Absolute analysis %		Which court is the information from?		
Break %		Horseferry	Milton	Newcastle-
Respondents	Base	Road	Keynes	under-Lyme
	2,320	7	1,862	451
	0.3%	80.3	19.4	%
Offences prosecuted				
by the DT/DVLA				
Driver and vehicle	2,308	7	1,851	450
licence offences	99.5%	100.0%	99.4%	99.8%
		0.3%	80.2%	19.5%
No trade/goods	11	0.0%	11	0.0%
operator's licence	0.5%	0.0%	0.6%	0.0%
			100.0%	
Obstructing a	1	0.0%	0.0%	1
police officer	0.0%	0.0%	0.0%	0.2%
			100.0%	
Other	0.0%	0.0%	0.0%	0.0%
		0.0%	0.0%	0.0%

driver and vehicle licence offences.

Eleven defendants (0.6 per cent) were prosecuted for not having a trade/ goods operator's licence. To a great extent this phenomenon reflects the urban geography of Milton Keynes in contradistinction from the London court in Horseferry Road and the old town court in Newcastle-under-Lyme. Milton Keynes was designed as a grid system of large freeway-style roads and roundabouts, with all shops, schools and residential areas set apart from this road system. Thus, virtually all the parking in Milton Keynes is in car parks which provide easy areas for anyone who wants to check vehicles (council officials, car park attendants, police officers and traffic wardens) to patrol.

At Newcastle-under-Lyme 451 (19.4 per cent) defendants were prosecuted by the DT/DVLA, 450 for driver and vehicle licence offences and one defendant for obstructing a police officer. Only seven defendants were prosecuted at Horseferry Road – all of them for driver and vehicle licence offences.

Pleas Of the 2,320 cases examined, there were 647 (27.9 per cent) guilty pleas and 46 (2.0 per cent) not guilty. One thousand four hundred and thirty-two (61.7 per cent) cases were recorded as 'no appearance' and 106 (4.6 per cent) not known (P1).

Verdicts One thousand eight hundred and fifty-three (79.9 per cent) defendants were convicted, there were none found not guilty and there was one remanded on bail. Two hundred and ten (9.1 per cent) cases were withdrawn/dismissed, 162 (7.0 per cent) adjourned, one warrant issued and 93 summons not served (P2).

Disposals Of the 1,853 convicted, 1,814 (97.9 per cent) were given a fine. One defendant was imprisoned, 15 (0.8 per cent) were remanded on bail, 21 (1.1 per cent) given an absolute discharge and two (0.1 per cent) a conditional discharge (P3).

Presence in court and representation Seventy (3.0 per cent) defendants were present in court, 1,930 (83.2 per cent) were not present and 227 (9.8 per cent) not known (P4). Eight (0.3 per cent) defendants were represented, 714 (30.8 per cent) were not, with 1,501 (64.9 per cent) not known (P5).

It is here easy to see why this type of offending can be regarded as something other than a criminal offence even though it is being dealt with in a criminal court and is followed by the possibility of a criminal sanction. Of the 2,320 DT/DVLA cases examined in this study, 80 per cent resulted in convictions, and, of these, 98 per cent resulted in a fine. Only 3 per cent of defendants turned up in court, and only 0.3 per cent were known to have legal representation. Whatever the objective seriousness of the offending, the process by which it is dealt with bears all the signs of a low-level procedural matter rather than something perhaps normally associated in the public consciousness with a criminal court. The near inevitability of the conviction and its invariable consequence – a fine – detract from the normal courtroom tension, argument and uncertainties associated with a criminal trial. In procedural terms, these matters seem more akin to the sanctioning of overdue library books through the levying of an automatic financial penalty.

TVLEO

The scale of violations in respect of TV licences is high. The number of people caught without licences in 1997 rose to a record 400,000, and licence evasion is now estimated to cost £149 million a year.[4] The number of annual prosecutions has remained similar since 1997 and it is worthy of note that 400,000 offenders is almost 1 per cent of the adult population of Britain (or more than one prosecution every two seconds of the working day).[5] TV licence surveillance is one of the biggest law enforcement operations in the country, employing more operatives than MI5 and netting more criminal prosecutions than drugs and burglary combined. In the quest to catch the licence evaders, a inspectors (known as 'inquiry officers') are given the status of de facto police, able to issue cautions and take evidence. Some 500 search warrants are issued each year, and hundreds of thousands of homes are searched.

This system, intended to fund the operation of the BBC, is enforced not only by a massive computer network and more than 600 field inspectors, but by a fleet of TV detector vans and handheld scanners, which can detect signals from the 'horizontal sweep' local oscillator in a television (this is the device that fine tunes incoming signals). This technology is now also capable of detecting what programme a viewer is watching. The head of field operations at the TVLEO has indicated that each year only a tiny fraction of defendants (perhaps 100) escape conviction.[6] These cases seem to involve bizarre situations. In one case, for example, a defendant marched into court with his twin brother and then claimed that the confession given to the inspectors on his doorstep was invalid because it had been obtained from the wrong man. The prosecution was discontinued.

In the present study, 920 defendants (9.5 per cent) were prosecuted under the Wireless and Telegraph Act 1949 for having no television licence. The majority 559 (60.8 per cent) were at Milton Keynes, 220 (23.9 per cent) at Horseferry Road and 141 (15.3 per cent) at Newcastle-under-Lyme.

Table 3.4   TVLEO prosecutions and the courts

Absolute analysis %		Which court is the information from?		
Break %		Horseferry	Milton	Newcastle-
Respondents	Base	Road	Keynes	under-Lyme
	920	220	559	141
		23.9%	60.8%	15.3%
Offences prosecuted				
by TVLEO				
No television	919	220	559	140
licence	99.9%	23.9%	60.8%	15.2%
		100.0%	100.0%	99.3%
Other	1	0.0%	0.0%	0.0%
	0.1%	0.0%	0.0%	100.0%
				0.7%

Pleas There were 203 (22.1 per cent) guilty pleas and 42 (7.8 per cent) not guilty. Four hundred and ninety-one (53.4 per cent cases recorded no appearance and 192 (20.9 per cent) were not known (P1).

Verdicts Of the 920 defendants prosecuted, 654 (71 per cent) were convicted. 165 (17.9 per cent) cases were withdrawn/dismissed, 83 (9.0 per cent) adjourned and 18 (2.0 per cent) summons nor served (P2).

Disposals Of the 654 convictions, the majority 643 (98.3 per cent) were given a fine. Six (0.9 per cent) were remanded on bail, three defendants were given a conditional discharge and two an absolute discharge.

Presence in court and representation The majority 632 (68.7 per cent) of defendants did not appear in court. Ten were recorded as present. Two hundred and sixty (28.3 per cent) were not known (P4). There was no record of any defendant being represented (P5).

The real conviction rate in respect of these cases would be considerably higher than that manifested in these data. This is because it is likely that many of the adjourned (83) cases would in time result in convictions. It is also worthy of note that the number of withdrawn or dismissed cases (9 per cent) was higher than the infinitesimally small number of those prosecuted who escape conviction according to the head of field operations at the TVLEO.[7] If the same proportion of TVLEO cases were withdrawn nationally in 1998 as were in the three courts in this study (9 per cent) then (9 per cent of 400,000) 36,000 people without licences would escape conviction, a number that is notably different from the 'tiny fraction' of about 100 estimated by the TVLEO's head of field operations.

DSS

Of the 527 defendants the DSS prosecuted (5.4 per cent of all cases in the study), *Horseferry Road* heard 257 (48.8 per cent), *Milton Keynes* 187 (35.5 per cent) and *Newcastle-under-Lyme* 83 (15.3 per cent).

Overall, 362 (68.7 per cent) of offences prosecuted were for dishonestly obtaining benefit under the Social Security Administration Act 1992; 147 (27.9 per cent) for dishonestly obtaining a jobseeker's allowance under the Jobseekers Act 1995; seven for false accounting, six for aiding and abetting the making of a false passport, and five for aiding and abetting one who dishonestly obtains money by deception.

Table 3.5   DSS prosecutions and the courts

Absolute analysis % Break % Respondents	Base	Which court is the information from?		
		Horseferry Road	Milton Keynes	Newcastle- under-Lyme
	527	257	187	83
		48.8%	35.5%	15.7%
Offences prosecuted **by DSS**				
Dishonestly	362	161	126	75
obtaining benefit	68.7%	44.5%	34.8%	20.7%
		62.6%	67.4%	90.4%
Dishonestly obtaining	147	83	61	3
a Jobseeker's Allowance	27.9%	56.5%.	41.5%	2.0%
		32.3%	32.6%	3.6%
Aiding and abetting one	5	0.0%	0.0%	5
who dishonestly obtained	0.9%	0.0%	0.0%	100.0%
monies by deception				6.0%
Aiding and abetting the	6	6	0.0%	0.0%
making of a false passport	1.1%	100.0%	0.0%	0.0%
		2.3%		
False accounting	7	7	0.0%	0.0%
	1.3%	100.0%	0.0%	0.0%
		2.7%		

Pleas Two hundred and thirty-three (44.2 per cent) of defendants pleaded guilty and 33 (6.3 per cent) not guilty. Sixty (11.4 per cent) of cases were recorded as no appearance and 195 (37.0 per cent) are not known (P1).

Verdicts Of the 527 prosecutions there were 217 (41.2 per cent) proved. One defendant was found not guilty and 184 (34.9 per cent) defendants were remanded on bail. Seventy-six (14.4 per cent) cases were adjourned, 11 (2.1 per cent) withdrawn/dismissed and there were 33 (6.3 per cent) warrants issued and five summons not served (P2).

Disposals Of the 217 defendants convicted, nine (4.1 per cent) were sent to prison, 32 (14.7 per cent) were given a fine, 52 (24 per cent) Community Service, 14 (6.5 per cent) Probation and eight (3.7 per cent) a Combination Order. Five (2.3 per cent) defendants were remanded in custody and 69 (31.8 per cent) remanded on bail. Twenty-seven (12.4 per cent) were given a conditional discharge and there was one sentence suspended (P3).

Presence in court and representation Two hundred and twenty-seven (43.1 per cent) of the defendants were present in court. Seventy-three (13.9 per cent) were recorded not present and 221 (41.9 per cent) not known (P4). Sixty-nine (13.1 per cent) of the defendants were represented, 14 (2.7 per cent) not represented and 437 (82.9 per cent) not known (P5).

Here, by contrast with some of the other types of non-CPS prosecution – like those brought by the TVLEO (above) – there is a much closer approximation to the case features of conventional crimes: nearly half of the defendants are pleading.

The Vehicle Inspectorate

Of the 535 prosecutions brought (5.5 per cent), Newcastle-under-Lyme accounted for 388 (72.5 per cent), Milton Keynes 134 (25. per cent) and Horseferry Road 13 (2.4 per cent) as is shown in Table 3.6.

The offences were prosecuted mostly under The Road Traffic Act 1988, Road Vehicle (Construction and Use) Regulations 1986, Road Vehicles (Registration and Licensing) Regulations 1971, Public Service Vehicles (Condition of Fitness, Equipment, Use and Certification) Regulations 1981 and the Road Traffic Offenders Act 1988. They were for either one or a combination of offences including gross weight excess, recording equipment irregularities, having no goods operator's licence, forging a test certificate, failing to observe a statutory break, failing to produce a record sheet, not affixing a ministry plate and/or test date disc and obstructing a public entrance.

At *Newcastle-under-Lyme*, of the offences prosecuted by the VI, most were for gross weight excess (184, 47.4 per cent) or for a combination of offences under Road Traffic Act/Regulations above (178, 45.9 per cent).

At *Milton Keynes* the main offence prosecuted was gross weight excess (64, 47.8 per cent), followed by 34 (25.4 per cent) for having no goods operator's licence.

Pleas Of the 535 defendants accused, 338 (63.2 per cent) pleaded guilty and 42 (7.8 per cent) not guilty. Eighty-three (15.5 per cent) were recorded no appearance and 71 (13.3 per cent) not known (P1).

Verdicts Three hundred and sixty (67.3 per cent) defendants were convicted, one was found not guilty and eight (1.5 per cent) were remanded on bail. One hundred and thirty-nine (26 per cent) cases were adjourned, 26 (4.9 per cent) were withdrawn/dismissed and there was one summons not served (P2).

Table 3.6   Vehicle Inspectorate prosecutions and the courts

Absolute analysis % Break % Respondents	Base	Which court is the information from? Horseferry Road	Milton Keynes	Newcastle-under-Lyme
	535	13 2.4%	134 25.0%	388 72.5%
Offences prosecuted by Vehicle Inspectorate				
Tachometer irregularities	37 6.9%	5 13.5% 38.5%	16 43.2% 11.9%	16 43.2% 4.1%
No goods operator's licence	40 7.5%	2 5.0% 15.4%	34 85.0% 25.4%	4 10.0% 1.0%
Forging a test certificate	5 0.9%	0.0% 0.0%	5 100.0% 3.7%	0.0% 0.0%
Failing to observe a statutory break	12 2.2%	6 50.0% 46.2%	6 50.0% 4.5%	0.0% 0.0%
Failing to produce a record sheet	8 1.5%	0.0% 0.0%	8 100.0% 6.0%	0.0% 0.0%
Ministry plate not affixed	3 0.6%	0.0% 0.0%	0.0% 0.0%	3 100.0% 0.8%
Test date disc not affixed	3 0.6%	0.0% 0.0%	0.0% 0.0%	3 100.0% 0.8%
Obstructing a public entrance	1 0.2%	0.0% 0.0%	1 100.0% 0.7%	0.0% 0.0%
Other	178 33.3%	0.0% 0.0%	0.0% 0.0%	178 100.0% 45.9%

Disposals Of the 360 defendants convicted, the vast majority 343 (95.3 per cent) were given a fine. Three (0.8 per cent) were remanded on bail and 14 (3.9 per cent) given an absolute discharge (P3).

Presence in court and representation Forty-eight (9 per cent) defendants were present in court, 391 (73.1 per cent) were not and 94 (17.6 per cent) were not known (P4). Fifty-two (9.7 per cent) were represented, 327 (61.1 per cent) not represented and 154 (28.8 per cent) not known (P5).

London Buses

Four hundred and twenty-seven (4.4 per cent) prosecutions were brought at *Horseferry Road.* Ninety-eight point one per cent (419) of the defendants were prosecuted for the offence of intent to avoid the payment of a fare or related offence. There were also five prosecutions for assault and three for disorderly conduct.

Table 3.7   London Buses prosecutions and the courts

Absolute analysis % Break % Respondents	Base	Which court is the information from?		
		Horseferry Road	Milton Keynes	Newcastle-under-Lyme
	427	427	0.0%	0.0%
Offences prosecuted by London Buses				
Intending to avoid payment of fare	419 98.1%	419 100.0% 98.1%	0.0% 0.0%	0.0% 0.0%
Assault	5 1.2%	5 100.0% 1.2%	0.0% 0.0%	0.0% 0.0%
Disorderly conduct	3 0.7%	3 100.0% 0.7%	0.0% 0.0%	0.0% 0.0%
Other	0.0%	0.0% 0.0%	0.0% 0.0%	0.0% 0.0%

Pleas There were 113 (26.5 per cent) pleas of guilty and 24 (5.6 per cent) of not guilty. One hundred and ten (25.8 per cent) cases recorded no appearance and 155 (36.3 per cent) were not known (P1).

Verdicts Two hundred and ninety-nine (70 per cent) defendants were convicted, one remanded on bail and one was remanded in custody. Fifty-six (13.1 per cent) cases were adjourned, 44 (10.3 per cent) withdrawn/dismissed one warrant issued and 25 (5.9 per cent) summons not served (P2).

Disposals Of those convicted the vast majority 292 (97.7 per cent) were fined. Five were absolutely discharged and two conditionally discharged (P3).

Presence in court and representation Eleven (2.6 per cent) defendants were present in court, 113 (26.5 per cent) were not and 278 (65.1 per cent) not known (P4). No defendants were recorded as being represented (P5).

SW Trains

The 271 prosecutions (2.8 per cent) brought by SW Trains at *Horseferry Road* were for the offence of intending to avoid payment of a fare or a related offence.

Pleas Eighty-seven (32.1 per cent) defendants pleaded guilty and 17 (6.3 per cent) not guilty. Seventy-eight (28.8 per cent) were recorded no appearance and there were 79 (29.2 per cent) not known (P1).

Verdicts One hundred and eighty-nine (69.7 per cent) of the defendants were convicted. There were 24 (9.8 per cent) cases withdrawn/dismissed and 47 (17.3 per cent) adjourned. One warrant was issued and one summons not served (P2).

Disposals Most of the defendants 187 (98.9 per cent) were given a fine. There were two conditional discharges (P3).

Presence in court and representation Seven (2.6 per cent) defendants appeared in court, 75 (27.7 per cent) were recorded not present and 180 (66.4 per cent) were not known (P4). None were recorded as represented (P5).

Inland Revenue

The Inland Revenue's primary function is as a debt collecting agency and prosecution is then used to assist with this function. The overall total of 210 (2.2 per cent) defendants were summoned before *Milton Keynes* Magistrate Court for failing to pay a sum of money recoverable as a civil debt.

Pleas The vast majority of the defendants 206 (98.1 per cent) did not appear in court. Only one defendant entered a plea of guilty (three were not known) (P1).

Verdicts Of the 210 cases, three (1.4 per cent) were convicted. One hundred and twenty (57.1 per cent) cases were adjourned and 87 (41.4 per cent) withdrawn or dismissed (P2).

Disposals Of the three convicted, two were fined and the third disposal had not been officially recorded in the Court Record (P3).

Presence in court and representation Three defendants were present in court (P4) and one defendant was recorded as being represented in court (P5).

Customs and Excise

One hundred and twenty-three prosecutions were recorded (1.3 per cent). One hundred and seven (87 per cent) were prosecuted at *Horseferry Road* and 16 (13 per cent) at *Milton Keynes.*

   At *Horseferry Road* the majority of defendants 95 (77.2 per cent) were charged importing prohibited drug. There were also 12 (11.2 per cent) offences of intent to defraud HM of duty payable on excise goods.

   At *Milton Keynes* there were 11 (68.8 per cent) offences of intent to defraud HM of duty payable on excise goods and five (31.3 per cent) offences of importing goods not 'for own use'.

Table 3.8   Customs and Excise prosecutions and the courts

Absolute analysis % Break % Respondents	Base	Which court is the information from?		
		Horseferry Road	Milton Keynes	Newcastle-under-Lyme
	123	107	16	0.0%
Offences prosecuted by Customs and Excise				
Intent to defraud	23	12	11	0.0%
HM of duty payable	18.7%	52.2%	47.8%	0.0%
on excise goods	11.2%	68.8%		
Importing goods not	5	0.0%	5	0.0%
'for own use'	4.1%	0.0%	100.0%	0.0%
		31.3%		
Other	0.0%	0.0%	0.0%	0.0%
		0.0%	0.0%	0.0%

Pleas Overall 31 (25.2 per cent) of the defendants pleaded guilty and 14 (11.4

per cent) pleaded not guilty. Twelve (9.8 per cent) were recorded as no appearance with 65 cases not known (P1).

Verdicts Fifteen (12.2 per cent) defendants were convicted, 76 (61.8 per cent) were remanded in custody and 17 (13.8 per cent) remanded on bail. Ten cases were adjourned, four withdrawn/dismissed and one summons not served (P2).

Disposals Of the 15 convicted, nine were fined, two imprisoned and one was remanded on bail. Two received a conditional discharge and one given a community service order (P3).

Presence in court and representation Eighty-one (65.9 per cent) of the defendants were present in court, 12 (9.8 per cent) were not and in 30 (24.4 per cent) cases it was not known (P4). Two defendants were recorded as being represented (P5).

Education Welfare

One hundred and eighteen (1.2 per cent) defendants were prosecuted under The Education Act 1996 for failing to ensure a child attends school regularly. Ninety-two (78 per cent) were at *Milton Keynes*, 24 (20.3 per cent) at *Newcastle-under-Lyme* and two (1.7 per cent) at *Horseferry Road*.

Table 3.9   Education Welfare prosecutions and the courts

Absolute analysis % Break % Respondents	Base	Which court is the information from?		
		Horseferry Road	Milton Keynes	Newcastle- under-Lyme
	118	2	92	24
		1.7%	78.0%	20.3%
Offences prosecuted by **Education Welfare**				
Failing to ensure a	118	2	92	24
child attends	100.0%	1.7%	78.0%	20.3%
school regularly		100.0%	100.0%	100.0%

Pleas Fifty-three (44.9 per cent) of the accused pleaded guilty and two (1.7 per cent) not guilty. Forty-three (36.4 per cent) cases recorded no appearance and 20 (16.9 per cent) not known (P1).

Verdicts Seventy-seven (65.3 per cent) were convicted and two (1.7 per cent) remanded on bail. Thirty-five (29.7 per cent) cases were adjourned and four withdrawn/dismissed (P2).

Disposals Of the 77 defendants convicted, 36 (46.8 per cent) were given a fine, seven (9.1 per cent) Probation and five (6.5 per cent) remanded on bail. There were 26 (33.8 per cent) conditional discharges and three (3.9 per cent) absolute discharges (P3).

Presence in court and representation Twenty-eight (23.7 per cent) of the accused were present in court, 50 (42.4 per cent) not present and 40 (33.9 per cent) not known (P4). Eleven (9.3 per cent) of the defendants were represented, 16 (13.6 per cent) not represented and 91 (77.1 per cent) not known (P5).

The Environment Agency

Of the 97 (1.0 per cent) offences prosecuted by the Environment Agency, 87 (89.7 per cent) were at *Newcastle-under-Lyme* and 10 (10.3 per cent) at *Milton Keynes*. All the defendants were prosecuted under the Salmon and Freshwater Fisheries Act 1995 for fishing without a rod licence.

Table 3.10   Environment Agency prosecutions and the courts

Absolute analysis % Break % Respondents	Base	Which court is the information from?		
		Horseferry Road	Milton Keynes	Newcastle-under-Lyme
	97	0.0%	10	87
Offences prosecuted by the Environment Agency				
Fishing without a	97	0.0%	10	87
rod licence	100.0%	0.0%	10.3%	89.7%
			100.0%	100.0%

Pleas Forty-three (44.3 per cent) of the defendants pleaded guilty. Thirty-four (35.1 per cent) were recorded no appearance and 16 not known (P1).

Verdicts The majority 72 (74.2 per cent) were convicted. Thirteen (13.4 per cent) cases were withdrawn/dismissed, six (6.2 per cent) adjourned and six (6.2 per cent) summons not served (P2).

Disposals Of those convicted, 69 (95.8 per cent) were given a fine, one was put on probation and two remanded on bail (P3).

Presence in court and representation Four (4.1 per cent) of the accused were present in court, 76 (78.4 per cent) not present and 11 (11.3 per cent) not known (P4). None of the defendants were recorded as present in court (P5).

Department of Trade and Industry

Of the 37 (0.4 per cent) prosecutions, 28 (75.7 per cent) were at *Horseferry Road*, eight (21.6 per cent) at *Milton Keynes* and one at *Newcastle-under-Lyme*.

At *Horseferry Road* 19 (67.9 per cent) defendants were prosecuted for business trading offences while a bankrupt, two (7.1 per cent) for failing to disclose a loan when in voluntary liquidation, five (17.9 per cent) for failing to produce documents for inspection under the Companies Act 1985 and there were two offences of accruing gambling losses to increase the extent of insolvency.

At *Milton Keynes* four defendants were accused of business trading offences while a bankrupt and there was one offence of obtaining credit while a bankrupt.

At *Newcastle-under-Lyme* there was offence of obtaining credit while a bankrupt.

Pleas Four defendants pleaded guilty, two not guilty. There were seven no appearance and 23 not known (P1).

Verdicts Five were convicted, 10 remanded on bail, five withdrawn, 15 adjourned, one warrant issued and one summons not served (P2).

Disposals One fine, one Community Service, two conditional discharges and one sentence suspended (P3).

Presence in court and representation Six defendants appeared in court, seven were not present, with 23 not known (P4). One defendant was represented (P5).

Department of Trading Standards

Of the 33 (0.3 per cent) cases prosecuted, 32 (97 per cent) were at *Newcastle-under-Lyme* and only one at *Milton Keynes* which was for selling counterfeit goods.

Table 3.11   DTI prosecutions and the courts

Absolute analysis % Break % Respondents	Base	Which court is the information from?		
		Horseferry Road	Milton Keynes	Newcastle-under-Lyme
	37	28	8	1
		75.7%	21.6%	2.7%
Offences prosecuted by DTI				
Obtaining credit while a bankrupt	2 5.4%	0.0% 0.0%	1 50.0% 12.5%	1 50.0% 100.0%
Business trading offences while a bankrupt	23 62.2%	19 82.6% 67.9%	4 17.4% 50.0%	0.0% 0.0%
Failing to disclose a loan when in voluntary liquidation	2 5.4%	2 100.0% 7.1%	0.0% 0.0%	0.0% 0.0%
Failing to produce documents for inspection required under Companies Act 1985	5 13.5%	5 100.0% 17.9%	0.0% 0.0%	0.0% 0.0%
Emitting noise amounting to a statutory nuisance	0.0%	0.0% 0.0%	0.0% 0.0%	0.0% 0.0%
Acting as insolvency practitioner when not qualified to act	0.0%	0.0% 0.0%	0.0% 0.0%	0.0% 0.0%
Accruing gambling losses to increase extent of insolvency	2 5.4%	2 100.0% 7.1%	0.0% 0.0%	0.0% 0.0%
Other	3 8.1%	0.0% 0.0%	3 100.0% 37.5%	0.0% 0.0%

Twenty-one (65.6 per cent) at Newcastle-under-Lyme were for making a false trade description of goods, six for removing 'sell by date' from goods, two for making a misleading advertisement of service provided, two for failing to remove a sheep's carcass without undue delay and one 'other' of supplying a vehicle with structural corrosion (Table 3.12).

Pleas Eleven guilty, 19 not guilty, one no appearance and one not known (P1).

Table 3.12   DTS prosecutions and the courts

Absolute analysis % Break % Respondents	Base	Which court is the information from? Horseferry Road	Milton Keynes	Newcastle-under-Lyme
	37	28	8	1
Offences prosecuted by DTS				
Making false trade description of goods	21 63.6%	0.0% 0.0%	0.0% 0.0%	21 100.0% 65.6%
Making a misleading advertisement of services provided	2 6.1%	0.0% 0.0%	0.0% 0.0%	2 100.0% 6.3%
Removing 'sell by' date from goods	6 18.2%	0.0% 0.0%	0.0% 0.0%	6 100.0% 18.8%
Failing to remove sheep's carcass without undue delay	2 6.1%	0.0% 0.0%	0.0% 0.0%	2 100.0% 6.3%
Selling counterfeit goods	1 3.0%	0.0% 0.0%	1 100.0% 100.0%	0.0% 0.0%
Other	1 3.0%	0.0% 0.0%	0.0% 0.0%	1 100.0% 3.1%

Verdicts Eighteen were convicted, eight remanded on bail, five adjourned and two withdrawn/dismissed (P2).

Disposals Seven fines, seven remanded on bail and four conditionally discharged (P3).

Presence in court and representation Twenty-five defendants were present, six not present and two not known (P4). One was represented (P5).

RSPCA

Of the 25 (0.3 per cent) of cases prosecuted, 17 (68 per cent) were at *Milton Keynes*, four at *Horseferry Road* and four at *Newcastle-under-Lyme*. All the offences were prosecuted under the Protection of Animals Act 1911 for causing unnecessary suffering to an animal (Table 3.13).

Table 3.13   RSPCA prosecutions and the courts

Absolute analysis %		Which court is the information from?		
Break %		Horseferry	Milton	Newcastle-
Respondents	Base	Road	Keynes	under-Lyme
	25	4	17	4
Offences prosecuted				
by RSPCA				
Causing unnecessary	25	4	17	4
suffering to	100.0%	16.0%	68.0%	16.0%
an animal		100.0%	100.0%	100.0%

Pleas Seven pleaded guilty, five not guilty, nine no appearance and four not known (P1).

Verdicts Seven convicted, six remanded on bail, one withdrawn/dismissed, nine adjourned, two warrants issued (P2).

Disposals One defendant was sent to prison and six were given a fine (P3).

Presence in court and representation Six were present in court, nine not present and 10 not known (P4). Four were represented, 21 not known (P5).

Electricity Supply Companies

The 18 (1.4 per cent) prosecutions were by the MEB at *Newcastle-under-Lyme* for offences under Road Traffic Regulations. (The MEB insures itself for motor insurance.)

Pleas Ten of no appearance recorded and eight unknown (P1).

Verdicts Five (27.8 per cent) defendants were convicted and two remanded on bail. Nine (50 per cent) cases were adjourned and two withdrawn/dismissed (P2).

Disposals The five convicted were remanded on bail (P3).

Presence in court and representation Two appeared in court, 10 not present and six not known (P4). Seven (38.9 per cent) were represented (P5).

Table 3.14   HSE prosecutions and the courts

Absolute analysis % Break % Respondents	Base	Which court is the information from?		
		Horseferry Road	Milton Keynes	Newcastle-under-Lyme
	15	7	1	7
		46.6%	6.7%	46.7%
Offences prosecuted by HSE				
Offences under	14	7	0.0%	7
HSWA 1974	93.3%	50.0%	0.0%	50.0%
		100.0%		100.0%
As an employer	1	0.0%	1	0.0%
being uninsured	6.7%	0.0%	100.0%	0.0%
			100.0%	
Other	0.0%	0.0%	0.0%	0.0%
		0.0%	0.0%	0.0%

HSE

Fifteen (0.2 per cent) defendants were prosecuted, seven (46.7 per cent) at *Horseferry Road* for offences under HSWA 1974, seven under the same Act at *Newcastle-under-Lyme* and one at *Milton Keynes* for being uninsured as an employer (Table 3.14).

Pleas Five (33.3 per cent) pleaded guilty, two no appearance and eight not known (P1).

Verdicts Seven (46.7 per cent) defendants were convicted and eight adjourned (P2).

Disposals Six (85.7 per cent) were given a fine and one remanded on bail (P3).

Presence in court and representation Three were present in court, five not present and seven not known (P4). Six (40 per cent) were represented, two not represented and seven not known (P5).

British Waterways

The 10 (0.1 per cent) prosecutions were brought at *Milton Keynes* under The

British Waterways Board Bye-laws 1976 for keeping a pleasure boat without a licence on a canal/river.

Pleas Six (60 per cent) pleaded guilty and four recorded no appearance (P1).

Verdicts Nine (90 per cent) were convicted and one withdrawn (P2).

Disposals The nine were all given a fine (P3).

Presence in court and representation None were present in court and none represented (P4 and P5).

Cab Law Enforcement

The six defendants were prosecuted at *Horseferry Road* for one offence of being guilty of misbehaviour as a cab driver, one for failing to wear his badge conspicuously, two for leaving the vehicle unlawfully and two for plying a cab for hire contrary to the licence.

Pleas Five pleaded guilty and one not guilty (P1).

Verdicts Five convicted, one withdrawn (P2).

Disposals The five were fined (P3).

Presence in court and representation One appeared and five were not known (P4). None were represented (P5).

BT Security (see Table 3.2)

The four prosecutions were at *Milton Keynes* for theft of money. There was one guilty plea, two no appearance and one not known. Three were convicted and one adjourned. One was given a fine, one remanded on bail and one conditionally discharged. One was present in court and none represented.

Department of Health

One defendant was prosecuted at *Horseferry Road* for possessing a product intended to be placed on the market without authorisation. The plea was not

Table 3.15   Pleas and the courts

Absolute analysis % Break % Respondents	Base	Which court is the information from?		
		Horseferry Road	Milton Keynes	Newcastle- under-Lyme
	9,688	3,211	5,225	1,252
		33.1%	53.9%	12.9%
What was the plea?				
Guilty	1,301	754	356	191
	13.4%	58.0%	27.4%	14.7%
		23.5%	6.8%	15.3%
Not guilty	320	194	103	32
	3.4%	59.0%	31.3%	9.7%
		6.0%	2.0%	2.6%
Guilty MCA	1,247	2	876	369
	12.9%	0.2%	70.2%	29.6%
		0.1%	16.8%	29.5%
Not guilty MCA	54	5	7	43
	0.6%	7.4%	13.0%	79.6%
		0.1%	0.1%	3.4%
No appearance	4,805	913	3,505	387
	49.6%	19.0%	72.9%	8.1%
		28.4%	67.1%	30.9%
Not known	1,593	1,102	271	220
	16.4%	69.2%	17.0%	13.8%
		34.3%	5.2%	17.6%
N/A	359	242	107	10
	3.7%	67.4%	29.8%	2.8%
		7.5%	2.0%	0.8%

guilty and the case was adjourned. The defendant was present in court but representation status is unknown.

Ministry of Agriculture

One defendant was prosecuted at *Horseferry Road* for falsifying an expenses claim form. The accused was present in court, pleaded guilty, was remanded on bail but representation status is unknown.

Pleas (see Table 3.15)

Of the 9,689 prosecutions examined, there were 2,548 (26.3 per cent) pleas of

Table 3.16 Verdicts and the courts

Absolute analysis % Break % Respondents	Base	Which court is the information from?		
		Horseferry Road	Milton Keynes	Newcastle- under-Lyme
	9.688	3,211	5,225	1,252
	33.1%	53.9%	12.9%	
Verdict				
Convicted/proved	6,555	1,969	3,686	900
	67.7%	30.0%	56.2%	13.7%
		61.3%	70.5%	71.9%
Not guilty	6	1	5	0.0%
	0.1%	16.7%	83.3%	
		0.0%	0.1%	
Withdrawn/	1,047	214	732	101
dismissed	10.8%	20.4%	69.9%	9.6%
		6.7%	14.0%	8.1%
Adjourned	1,343	573	584	186
	13.9%	42.7%	43.5%	13.8%
		17.8%	11.2%	14.9%
Warrant issued for	47	18	23	6
arrest	0.5%	38.3%	48.9%	12.8%
		0.6%	0.4%	0.5%
Summons not served	358	235	113	10
	3.7%	65.6%	31.6%	2.8%
		7.3%	2.2%	0.8%
Remanded in custody	81	79	2	0.0%
	0.8%	97.5%	2.5%	0.0%
		2.5%	0.0%	
Remanded on bail	251	122	80	49
	2.6%	48.6%	31.9%	19.5%
		3.8%	1.5%	3.9%
Emergency	0.0%	0.0%	0.0%	0.0%
prohibition order		0.0%	0.0%	0.0%

guilty, 383 (4 per cent) of not guilty, 4,845 (49.6 per cent) recorded no appearance, 1593 (16.4 per cent) not known and 359 (3.7 per cent) N/A (e.g. summons not served).

Verdicts (see Table 3.16)

Six thousand five hundred and fifty-five (67.7 per cent) were convicted/proved,

Table 3.17   Disposals and the courts

Absolute analysis % Break % Respondents	Base	Which court is the information from?		
		Horseferry Road	Milton Keynes	Newcastle- under-Lyme
	6,554	1,959	3,685	900
		30.0%	56.2%	13.7%
If convicted what was the disposal?				
Fine	6,146	1,849	3,480	817
	93.8%	30.1%	56.6%	13.3%
		93.9%	94.4%	90.8%
Remanded on bail	126	25	62	39
	1.9%	19.8%	49.2%	31.0%
		1.3%	1.7%	4.3%
Remanded in custody	5	1	0.0%	4
	0.1%	20.0%	0.0%	80.0%
		0.1%		0.4%
Imprisonment	14	11	2	1
	0.2%	78.6%	14.3%	7.1%
		0.6%	0.1%	0.1%
Probation	22	11	4	7
	0.3%	50.0%	18.2%	31.8%
		0.6%	0.1%	0.8%
Community Service	56	26	24	6
	0.9%	46.4%	42.9%	10.7%
		1.3%	0.7%	0.7%
Combination Order	8	2	1	5
	0.1%	25.0%	12.5%	62.5%
		0.1%	0.0%	0.6%
Absolute discharge	80	12	60	8
	1.2%	15.0%	75.0%	10.0%
		0.6%	1.6%	0.9%
Conditional discharge	95	31	51	13
	1.4%	32.6%	53.7%	13.7%
		1.6%	1.4%	1.4%
Sentence suspended	2	1	1	0.0%
	0.0%	50.0%	50.0%	0.0%
		0.1%	0.0%	

Table 3.18   Presence in court of defendants

Absolute analysis % Break % Respondents	Base	Which court is the information from?		
		Horseferry Road	Milton Keynes	Newcastle- under-Lyme
	9,688	3,211 33.1%	5,225 53.9%	1,252 12.9%
Was the 'accused' present in court?				
Yes	640 6.6%	239 37.3% 7.4%	198 30.9% 3.8%	203 31.7% 16.2%
No	6,232 64.3%	950 15.2% 29.6%	4,400 70.6% 84.2%	882 14.2% 70.4%
Not known	2,475 25.5%	1,805 72.9%	514 20.8%	156 6.3%
N/A	341 3.5%	217 63.6% 6.8%	113 33.1% 2.2%	11 3.2% 0.9%

Table 3.19   Representation and defendants

Absolute analysis % Break % Respondents	Base	Which court is the information from?		
		Horseferry Road	Milton Keynes	Newcastle- under-Lyme
	9,687	3,210 33.1%	5,225 53.9%	1,252 12.9%
Was the 'accused' represented in court?				
Yes	203 2.1%	8 3.9% 0.2%	6 3.0% 0.1%	189 93.1% 15.1%
No	1,729 17.8%	33 1.9% 1.0%	828 47.9% 15.8%	868 50.2% 69.3%
Not known	7,410 76.5%	2,949 39.8% 91.9%	4,277 57.7% 81.9%	184 2.5% 14.7%
N/A	345 3.6%	220 63.8% 6.9%	114 33.0% 2.2%	11 3.2% 0.9%

six (0.1 per cent) found not guilty, 251 (2.6 per cent) remanded on bail, 81 (0.8 per cent) remanded in custody, 47 (0.5 per cent) warrants issued, 1,047 (10.8 per cent) withdrawn/dismissed, 1,343 (13.9 per cent) adjourned and 358 (3.7 per cent) summons not served.

Disposals (see Table 3.17)

Six thousand one hundred and forty-six (93.8 per cent) were given a fine, 14 (0.2 per cent) sent to prison, 126 (1.9 per cent) remanded on bail, five (0.1 per cent) remanded in custody, 22 (0.3 per cent) put on probation, 56 (0.9 per cent) given Community Service, eight (0.1 per cent) given a Combination Order, 80 (1.2 per cent) an absolute discharge, 95 (1.4 per cent) a conditional discharge and two a suspended sentence.

Accused Present in Court (see Table 3.18)

Six hundred and forty (6.6 per cent) were present in court, 6,232 (64.3 per cent) not present, 2,475 (25.5 per cent) were not known and 341 (3.5 per cent) N/A.

Accused Represented in Court (see Table 3.19)

Two hundred and three (2.1 per cent) were represented, 1,729 (17.8 per cent) not represented, 7,410 (76.5 per cent) not known and 345 (3.6 per cent) N/A.

Notes

1   Annual Report of Her Majesty's Chief Inspector of the Magistrates' Court Service 1998/ 99, p. 4.
2   The conviction rate for magistrates courts in 1997 was 70 per cent – Information on the Criminal Justice System in England and Wales, Digest 4, Home Office Research Development Study, October 1999, p. 35.
3   Ibid., p. 39.
4   *Daily Telegraph*, 5 August 2000.
5   Simon Davies, *The Daily Telegraph*, 9 April 1998. I am indebted to Mr Davies for much of the introductory data.
6   Ibid.
7   Ibid.

Chapter Four

The Magistrates' Clerks Survey

There are 400 magistrates' courts in England and Wales. For the purposes of adding a substantive and qualitative dimension to this research, 100 justices' clerks were written to with a questionnaire and an invitation to make general comments and observations about different aspects of the non-CPS prosecutorial process (see Magistrates' Survey, Appendix 3). The response rate was 68 per cent. The courts were chosen to represent the variety of jurisdictions across the country – metropolitan and rural courts, inland courts and coastal courts, old towns and new towns and courts from the north, south east and west.

The position of the clerk to the justices is key to the functioning of the court and it was thus seen as of critical importance to the research to discover how non-CPS prosecutions were seen and experienced by those who legally managed the court. Clerks to the justices give legal advice to the lay magistrates both inside and out of the court, and cultivate a relationship with magistrates to ensure that their advice is respected. On the administrative side, their duties include accounting for fines and fees; and line management for non-legal and specialist staff. As clerks sit across the full range of cases, they will be able to develop a view about the efficiency of both CPS and non-CPS prosecutions, and to compare and contrast the ways in which these two sorts of prosecution are handled in terms both of case-management and advocacy.

I turn now to look in a little more detail at the role of the justices' clerk, and I am indebted to the Lord Chancellor's Department for its work on this subject which I rely on here.

The Justices' Clerk

Justices' clerks have been influential contributors to the criminal justice system for a very long time. As the Lord Chancellor's Department noted (Lord Chancellor's Department, 1998, para. 4) over the last 50 years or so, the duties and functions of the post have developed organically: there have been many changes to the organisation and functions of magistrates courts, often without a clear view or vision of the overall framework or structure being created. At the time of writing the government is embarking on a fresh approach. Ministers have made it clear they wanted to see a much more strategic and 'joined up' system of all the criminal justice agencies. For magistrates' courts, this means (Lord Chancellor's Department, 1998, para. 6):

> a programme of amalgamation of Magistrates' Courts Committees (MCCs), moving towards fewer and larger committees which align their boundaries with those of other criminal justices agencies;

> a more strategic approach to the use of resources across the whole system;

> a greater separation of the legal and administrative functions undertaken; and

> better and more flexible use of professional and judicial resources.

Statutory Position of Justices' Clerks

Justices' clerks may be employed by MCCs only after their candidature has been approved by the Lord Chancellor in accordance with section 42 of the Justices of the Peace Act 1997. In addition, and now in wholly exceptional circumstances only, one person may hold the dual appointment of justices' chief executive and justices' clerk with the Lord Chancellor's agreement in accordance with section 40(6) of the Justices of the Peace Act 1997 (Guidance on Appointment of Justices' Chief Executives and Justices' Clerks) was issued on 1 April 1998. Section 45 of the Justices of the Peace Act 1997, particularly subsections (4) and (5), serves to clarify the primary role of the justices' clerk as legal adviser; and section 48 of the Justices of the Peace Act 1997 sets out the independence of justices' clerks and staff in relation to legal functions.

Today, the justices' chief executive is the line manager for all staff employed by the MCC, including justices' clerks. Under the direction and leadership of the chief executive, it is the staff of the MCC to whom most tasks are delegated. The government supports the view that so long as proper directions are given, and the person undertaking the task is considered capable, any task that is not restricted to a specified person by statute, may be delegated. Delegating the task in question does not mean that the person in whom the task is statutorily or otherwise vested, relinquishes overall accountability.

The government has stated (Lord Chancellor's Department, 1998, 2(ii)) that it is in favour of greater separation of the legal and administrative functions. One of the main considerations underlying ministers' policy on a greater separation between legal and administrative functions in magistrates' courts, is that the primary role of the justices' clerk to provide the best possible advice and support to magistrates. The Lord Chancellor's Department has averred (ibid.) that the primary role 'should neither be compromised nor diluted'. Ministers announced in a Statement to both Houses of Parliament on 29 October 1997 that when a suitable legislative opportunity arises they will transfer the statutory responsibility for the fines and fees accounts to the justices' chief executive. The government sees that as an important step towards the policy of greater separation.

Ministerial policy is one aimed at greater professionalisation of the status of the justices' clerk. On 11 August 1998 it was announced by the Lord Chancellor's Department that from 1 January 1999, all new justices' clerks appointed shall be professionally qualified as a solicitor or barrister. There will be a 10 year transition for existing justices' clerks, with special arrangements for those unqualified justices' clerks near retirement age. The vision for the next century is therefore a wholly professionalised legal support service for the lay magistracy.

The Crime and Disorder Act 1998 extends the range of functions that may be delegated from magistrates to clerks. These powers were intended to allow better case management, so that delays in magistrates' courts can be kept to a minimum. Ministers consider it appropriate that clerks should undertake preliminary case management in order to ensure that cases are progressed as quickly as possible and that the bench hears cases that are ready – although some areas prefer to use single justices for this work, not least because the powers available to single justices at preliminary hearings are more extensive.

This potential extension of clerks' powers does not alter the clerks' traditional role of providing the advice and support necessary to the bench. It is important to remember that the powers exercised by clerks are delegated powers from single justices. The government has expressed a wish (Lord Chancellor's Department, 1998, 2 (v)(20)) to see operating effectively in supporting the bench and to ensure that it is open for them to provide more assistance in managing cases effectively. Given their legal qualifications and training, and their extensive court and professional experience, ministers see this legal and expert advisory and supporting role as being the main focus for clerks.

The Need for a National Framework

There is currently no single definition of the duties for which a justices' clerk should be responsible. Similarly no national guidelines exist. Each MCC is responsible not only for employing its staff, but also determining the service provided locally. However, with this freedom, the Lord Chancellor's Department (1997, 2 (vi)(21)) notes, 'vast differences have emerged in individual responsibilities and the organisational model within MCCs'. Ministers have received an increasing number of representations, for example, as to which model is preferred and whether there is a national strategy, or commenting on the recruitment and appointment processes undertaken by other MCCs. The Lord Chancellor's Department has said that 'it has become clear that a strategic steer is needed' (ibid.).

Ultimately, it remains for the relevant magistrates' courts committee to decide how it will use its resources to provide that local service.

General Comments about the Questionnaire Format

The survey consisted of a self-report questionnaire on a Likert-style format on a scale of one to five:

1 = disagree strongly;
2 = disagree a little;
3 = undecided;
4 = agree a little;
5 = agree strongly.

The responses were generally very diligently completed. Two magistrates commented that they would have liked an 'agree' category between 4 and 5. Seven respondents found the questions too broad and difficult to answer because of their generality and the wide range of offences involved, for example, from cruelty to animals and Customs & Excise cases to TV licence cases. An eighth magistrate commented that the questions are meaningless outside a specific context and his replies were based on generality. He stated that there is no 'system' of non-police prosecution.

Analysis by Question

Q1   The Enforcement of the Relevant Parts of the Criminal Law is Fulfilled Satisfactorily by Non-police Prosecuting Agencies

The majority of replies 57 (83.8 per cent) agreed with the statement – 38 (55.9 per cent) agreed a little and 19 (27.9 per cent) agreed strongly. Eight (11.8 per cent) disagreed a little, none disagreed strongly. Three (4.4 per cent) were undecided.

It should thus be noted from the outset that, from the point of view of those legally advising the lay bench about law and procedure, the dramas that unfold in front of them in the form of multifarious prosecuting agencies are working satisfactorily with nearly 84 per cent. The implications for social policy could thus be regarded from one of three principal perspectives: that no substantial changes are required to the *status quo*; that no systemic changes are required although some limited, compartmentalised changes would improve the operation of the current system; or that the acquiescence of justices' clerks in the *status quo* does not necessarily mean that the system is working in the best interests of a wider constituency like those in 'the criminal justice system' or 'the justice system' or 'society at large'.

Q2   Non-police Prosecutions are an Efficient Way of Securing General Compliance with the Legislation

Again the majority 52 (76.5 per cent) agreed with the statement – 35 (51.5 per cent) agreed a little and 17 (25 per cent) agreed strongly. Six (8.8 per cent) disagreed a little and two (2.9 per cent) disagreed strongly. Eight (11.8 per cent) were undecided. There is a considerable range of relevant legislation here, so, clearly, responses engage at a broad level of generalisation. Thus, these responses are quite consistent with a state of affairs where there could be a significant difference between the efficacy of the various agencies. For instance, most respondents could, consistent with this result, believe that one or two of the non-CPS agencies are not good at securing compliance with the relevant legislation. Nonetheless, as with the responses to question one, there is from the point of view of the legal court manager, a clear endorsement of the current system.

*Q3   There is a Social Importance in the Function and Powers they
       Possess*

The majority 50 (73.5 per cent) agreed with the statement – 31 (45.6 per cent) strongly and 19 (27.9 per cent) a little. Fourteen (20.6 per cent) were undecided. One magistrate disagreed strongly and one a little. There were two 'no reply' responses to this question. In the debate and discussion organised by the Royal Commission on Criminal Procedure (1978) one issue was whether it would be preferable to bring under one national prosecuting agency responsibility for all prosecutions (i.e. police, local government, government departments, vehicle licensing, HSE, TV licensing, RSPCA etc.) or whether, alongside an agency to prosecute ordinary crime, the multifarious organisations should also be permitted to use their own accrued special expertise to bring their own cases. In the event, the Prosecution of Offences Act 1985 set up the Crown Prosecution Service and did leave private and organisational prosecutions to be pursued separately.

*Q4   Although the Investigative and Prosecutorial Roles in Non-police
       Agency Cases is Often Performed by the Same Organisation, the
       System Works Well*

The majority 54 (79.3 per cent) agreed with the statement – 33 (48.5 per cent) agreed a little and 21 (30.9 per cent) agreed strongly. Eight (11.8 per cent) were undecided. Four (5.9 per cent) disagreed a little and two (2.9 per cent) disagreed strongly. This profile of opinion is of particular interest in the context of criminal justice policy of the last 20 years. In short, the CPS was formed in order to separate policing from prosecution but 15 years on the experience of the public, the professions and government has led to a partial reversion to the old system as Crown prosecutors and police officers are being put into local Criminal Justice Units to create a closer working relationship between the two services.

One of the most prominent reasons for the establishment of the CPS was the perceived need to separate the investigative and prosecutorial roles historically both performed by the police. It was thought that the old system raised too great a danger that police officers, who had investigated a crime and charged a suspected culprit, might not in many cases have sufficient detachment to form a balanced view of the weight of the evidence. A report from JUSTICE (the British Section of the International Commission of Jurists) (JUSTICE, 1970) argued that the police were not best suited to be prosecutors because they would have a commitment to winning a case even when the actual evidence was weak (JUSTICE, 1970, p. 5):

> The honest, zealous and conscientious police officer who has satisfied himself that the suspect is guilty becomes psychologically committed to prosecution and thus to successful prosecution. He wants to prosecute and he wants to win. As Sir Alexander Cockburn, then Attorney-General, put it (giving evidence to the Select Committee on Public Prosecutors in 1856) – when the police 'mix themselves up in the conduct of a prosecution ... they acquire a bias infinitely stronger than that which must under any circumstances naturally attach itself to their evidence'. In consequence, a senior police officer may be inhibited in refusing to prosecute in order not to damage police morale – whereas an independent prosecutor would not be influenced by such considerations.

They were also not best placed, it was argued, to consider any public policy aspects inherent in the discretion to prosecute:

> The decision to prosecute ... is not an easy one. It is by no means in every case where a law officer considers that a conviction might be obtained that it is thought desirable to prosecute. Sometimes there are reasons of public policy which make it undesirable to prosecute the case. Perhaps the prosecution would enable him [the defendant] to present himself as a martyr. Or perhaps he is too ill to attend his trial without great risk to his health or even to his life. All these factors enter into the consideration (Sir Elwyn Jones, Attorney-General, cited in JUSTICE, 1970, 7(b)).

The JUSTICE report notes that, at that time, the English system was the only one in Europe where the interrogation of suspects, the interviewing of witnesses, the gathering and testing of scientific evidence, the selection of evidence to be laid before the court, the decision as to what charges will be brought and the conduct of the prosecution were all under the control of the police.

The report concluded with the following observation and recommendation (JUSTICE, 1970, pp. 12–13):

> ... the time has come for the appropriate changes to be made and that a system of public prosecution broadly following the lines of the Scottish system should be introduced ... Accordingly, the Committee recommends:
> (a) that there should be established a Department of Public Prosecutions to be responsible both for the decision to prosecute and for the conduct of the prosecutions.

The Crown Prosecution Service was not created until 1985. However, after 15 years of CPS operation, lack of communication between the police and CPS prosecutors was seen by many (especially some police officers who, distressed at the number of case files they submit which are not prosecuted, have dubbed the CPS the 'Criminal Protection Society') as problematic. In an attempt to improve liaison between the police investigating a case and the CPS, a pilot scheme, launched in several police stations in 1996, put a CPS officer with a desk in the police station. The government then resolved to introduce such 'Criminal Justice Units' on a national basis.

In June 2000, the CPS launched what it termed the start of a 'revolution' in prosecuting crime. Lord Williams of Mostyn, the Attorney-General, opened the first of many new Justice Units the government plans to establish in the future across England and Wales (http://tap.ccta.gov.uk/cps/infoupdate3). The Units were a key recommendation of Sir Iain Glidewell in his report on the CPS in 1998. For the first time since the service was established in 1986, Crown Prosecutors and the police will work together on cases in the same office.

The reforms will see a return to the principle of police and lawyers working on a case together. The first units will be set up in Avon and Somerset: a trials unit, to handle serious crimes, is being established at the CPS offices in Bristol and a criminal justice unit, based in police accommodation, to handle the magistrates' court cases. In place of duplicate police and CPS files for 30,000 magistrates' court cases will be a single file for each case on which both lawyer and police officer will work.

The trials unit will be staffed by 41 CPS and 10 police staff, and will handle 3,000 serious Crown Court cases a year. The Director of Public Prosecutions, David Calvert-Smith QC has stated that the new system will see:

> police detectives and senior prosecution lawyers working more closely on serious casework such as rape, armed robbery and murder. CPS lawyers will be on hand at the outset of police inquiries to advise senior officers on legal aspects of investigations and subsequently prepare cases for Crown Court (*The Times*, 27 June 2000).

David Archer, CPS chief prosecutor for Avon and Somerset, has observed that the old system operated on the basis that the police would build a file, then copy it to the CPS – a process repeated in 30,000 cases a year. All the evidence and witness statements were similarly copied, and sent off to the CPS under separate cover. Notifying witnesses would also be carried out as a paper exercise, through the post. Technology will now enable instant updating of files with investigating officers instantly e-mailed. They in turn will be able to e-mail immediate replies to CPS lawyers.

Under the new system, the police still retain the decision to charge. Even so, the architects of the innovation hope that the police will more readily ask prosecutors for legal advice before charge, and thereby reduce the likelihood of cases being discontinued at a later stage.

Neil Addison, a barrister and former prosecutor, has acknowledged that closer links will cut costs.

> Administration between CPS and the police has been the major weakness in the way the CPS was set up. I've always taken the view that they do have to work together ... it is unrealistic to think they can work in self-contained cocoons (ibid.).

There are, however, still serious misgivings in some quarters about such close liaison between police and prosecuting lawyers. Bruce Houlder QC, vice-chairman of the Criminal Bar Association, has stated that anxiety in this way: '... I am always worried about CPS officials working in police stations because it is too easy to fall into a police culture.'

Some defence lawyers and prosecutors are worried about a return to the 'bad old days' before the CPS as during the 1970s and 1980s many suspects were wrongly convicted because strong evidence proving their innocence was deliberately disregarded. There is concern that under the new system, with lawyers and police officers working in the same office the police could pressurise prosecution lawyers into taking flawed cases to court. Malcolm Fowler, chairman of the Law Society's criminal law committee has suggested that 'the problem is when the police develop a case theory for the crime and then only present evidence which fits that theory'.

The experience of magistrates' justices' clerks is clearly that the systems in which investigative and prosecutorial functions are discharged by a single agency works satisfactorily. One can surmise that the clerks' view would be different if they saw a significant number of non-CPS cases in which, through an overzealous approach to prosecution cases often collapsed or were rebutted by good defence lawyers in ways which suggested that non-CPS prosecutors were bending the rules or disregarding evidence in order to obtain convictions.

Q5   There is a Marked Contrast between the Police Approach and that of the Agencies in Relation to Investigation and Prosecution of Offences

The majority 46 (67.7 per cent) agreed with the statement, 28 (41.2 per cent) a little and 18 (26.5 per cent) strongly. Twelve (17.6 per cent) were undecided. Eight (11.8 per cent) disagreed a little and two (2.9 per cent) disagreed strongly.

It is of note here that nearly 70 per cent of justices' clerks agreed that the approach of the police in relation to the prosecution of what is commonly seen as 'ordinary crime' is different from the approach taken by the authorities in respect of regulatory offences.

With such a diversity of authorities prosecuting offences, there is, as Samuels (1986, p. 43) has observed, an element of injustice in there being different operating prosecutorial policies depending upon which agency is responsible for prosecuting. He notes that:

> The practices of the non-police agencies are diverse, different, variable, often there is no coherent policy within the agency, and there is certainly no coherent policy for all the agencies.

He goes on to note that some non-police agencies appear quick to prosecute, e.g. Social Security Fraud (though withdrawal of benefit and deduction from benefit are the most common remedies); others seem slow to prosecute using the threat, e.g. the Revenue. Some are concerned to promote good working standards, seeing prosecution as a last resort, e.g. the Health and Safety at Work Inspectorate.

The point is that the diversity of practice raises important questions of public interest and social justice. For example, many tax frauds are non prosecuted, whereas thefts from shops are (Research Study No. 10, S.Uglow, 'defending the public purse' [1984] Crim.L.R.128–141).

Samuels suggests (1986, p. 37) that:

> Settling by agreement and the imposition of penalties are extensively practised by the Revenue, but not the television authorities. The practice has the merit of getting the money in, avoiding the time, trouble and expense of prosecution, and avoiding publicity for the offender (if that be a merit).

Thus it can be proposed that the patchwork of prosecutorial practices which covers the full range of non-CPS cases is justified by reference to the significantly different ways in which the various agencies can best meet their separate objectives. Writing before the establishment of the CPS Samuels asked (1986, p. 38):

> Will the crown prosecution service be so effective and efficient that it will gradually grow and absorb the non-police work, so as ultimately to obtain the

forensic monopoly by statute? Or will the non-police agencies, or some of them, maintain and ever enhance the position as prosecuting agencies, because of the number of offences involved, their relatively minor character, and the variety, diversity and specialisation involved?

The answer to Samuel's question is that, 14 years later, the non-police agencies have survived and their workload, at least measured in reference to legislative duties and the range of regulations they must enforce, has grown. It should be noted, however, that according to the responses to question 8 (below) there does not appear to have been a significant rise in the non-CPS case load passing through the courts.

Interestingly, from the point of view of those who legally manage the affairs of the magistrates' courts (which deal with 95 per cent of all prosecutions), there is: (a) a marked difference between the prosecutorial approach of police and non-police prosecutions (according to 67.7 per cent of respondents to question 5): and (b) this duality is (according to 76.5 per cent of respondents to question 2) one which allows for the securing of an efficient securing of compliance with legislation. Thus it could be argued that although there is some injustice in the criminal justice system operating different standards of readiness to prosecute upon the detection of an offence (depending upon the nature of the wrong), a greater justice is served by permitting such differential readiness to prosecute. Such notions of justice are widely accepted, after all, in many other social spheres. Most parents and guardians, for example, accept that it is right in bringing up children to use some form of punishment when circumstances require (even if there is deep and passionate disagreement among adults about the most appropriate form that punishment should take) but accept also that, depending upon the nature of the wrong committed by a child, the imposition of a punishment might vary from almost automatic to a last resort option.

Q6 The Level of Resources Available to Non-police Agencies to Investigate and Prosecute is Adequate

Thirty-six (52.9 per cent) of magistrates were undecided about the proposition. Twenty-two (33.3 per cent) disagreed – 19 (27.9 per cent) a little and three (4.4 per cent) strongly. Eight (11.8 per cent) agreed a little and two (2.9 per cent) agreed strongly.

The preponderant opinion of justices' clerks in response to this issue seems to be at variance with the view of many people in non-CPS prosecuting agencies, and many outside observers. There is hard evidence to suggest that many agencies are woefully underfunded in the context of the extent of their responsibilities. Consider, for example, the work of the Health and Safety Executive. Evidence submitted to the House of Commons Select Committee on the Environment, Transport and Regional Affairs (Environment Sub Committee) (SCETRA, 1999) suggests that only a tiny fraction of possible violations of the Health and Safety at Work etc. Act 1974 are investigated, and an even smaller fraction prosecuted. Using data taken from official HSE reports, the Centre for Corporate Accountability showed that between 1996–98 there were 47,803 major injuries suffered in the workplace but the HSE failed to investigate in 89 per cent of these cases (ibid., p. 41). In these cases, the HSE also failed to prosecute in 89 per cent of cases. The decision as to whether it is appropriate to prosecute can only be made, of course, after a proper investigation. This record compares very unfavourably with that of the police who respond to and investigate all cases of serious injury. The Metropolitan Police, for example, categorise certain reports as 'incidents requiring immediate response'. This definition includes any reports of 'serious injury to people' (ibid., p. 44, para. 16). The major injuries reported to the HSE are just as likely to be the result of criminal conduct (having resulted from violation of the Health and Safety at Work etc. Act 1974) as the injuries which are defined as requiring immediate response by the police. In fact, the HSE in its own evidence submitted to the House of Commons' committee averred that:

> Prosecutions take up inordinate amounts of Inspectors' time, legal costs are not recovered by the HSE … and the penalties levied by the courts are often nugatory. Coupled with the effective prohibition on enforcement by anyone but Inspectors, the current system of enforcement is woefully inadequate (ibid., p. 36, para. 11).

The position of the Environment Agency is another case in point. The Agency's Annual Report 2000 reveals that inspections of waste sites and discharges were almost 20 per cent below planned levels in 1999/2000, and illegal waste operations were inadequately policed. The report shows almost 23,000 fewer inspections of licensed waste sites were carried out in 1999/2000 than the previous year, a drop (from 149,022 to 126,237) of 15 per cent, and significantly below the target of 150,000, while checks on waste carriers were at barely half of the previous year's level. Another big change in policing activity was a further 10 per cent reduction in inspections of discharges to water. Such inspections have been cut by almost 30,000 during the period

1998–2000 and were 24,000 below target in 1999. Clearly, any hope that the true level of criminal harm to the environment is being detected and prosecuted at appropriate levels is dashed by such data. Overall, the number of inspections in the main waste and pollution functions has declined by almost one-fifth in the period 1998–2000 (ENDS Report 308, September, 2000, p.10).

Similar evidence is to be found in a report of the Environment Sub-Committee of the House of Commons. It notes that:

> The overall perception has been that progress in creating an effective, coherent and confident new body has not been as rapid in the 32 years since the Agency was formed as it ought to have been.

The report also hints at underfunding in relation to staff pay:

> We further recommend that the Agency's pay system be urgently reviewed, with a view to ensuring that it encourages staff motivation and morale and thus Agency effectiveness.

One caveat in interpreting the responses to this question concerns the wide variety or non-CPS agencies involved in private prosecutions. While some like the HSE, and the Environment Agency are clearly underfunded in relation to what they are expected to do, the is no evidence that other organisations like the Inland Revenue or Customs and Excise are awkwardly limited in what they need to do by inadequate resources.

Q7   Non-police Prosecutions Contribute Significantly to Magistrates' Courts' Workloads

The majority 36 (53 per cent) agreed with the statement – 22 (32.4 per cent) agreed a little and 14 (20.6 per cent) agreed strongly. Twenty-one (30.9 per cent) also disagreed a little and 10 (14.7 per cent) disagreed strongly.

Between 20 per cent and 25 per cent of all cases coming before the criminal courts are prosecutions by agencies other than the CPS, and almost all of these are dealt with by the magistrates' courts (Samuels, 1986, p. 35).

At the time of the the Royal Commission study (Lidstone et al., 1980), the Home Office did attempt to collect data on the number of non-police prosecutions in England and Wales. The figure however was, by the admission of the Home Office, inaccurate because the data it received from police forces (who were responsible for collecting the figures from the magistrates' courts) were unreliable. The Royal Commission research team compared their findings in the 12 courts studied with the official figures available from the Home Office and found that (Lidstone et al., 1980, p. 31) the real figure of non-police prosecutions is likely to be about 2.1 times the official figure. The authors estimated that the proportion of non-juvenile, non-traffic cases which were brought by non-police prosecutions in 1977 was 27.4 per cent (ibid.).

The almost even split in this survey between justices' clerks who believe non-CPS work in their courts to be of a significant level and those who do not, should probably be accounted for by reference to the fact that magistrates' courts have quite different profiles of cases depending upon their location (rural, inner city, new town, coastal etc.) and demographic factors within their jurisdiction (impoverished urban populations generate high workloads of TV licence and DSS cases; and cases involving lorries are sometimes concentrated in particular geographic areas).

Q8   Non-police Prosecutions are Increasing Considerably

A majority of 28 (41.2 per cent) disagreed with the statement – 15 (22.1 per cent) disagreed strongly and 13 (19.1 per cent) a little. Twenty-two (32.4 per cent) were undecided. Seventeen (25 per cent) agreed a little and one agreed strongly.

During the last 15 years there has been a substantial increase in the range of legislation and delegated legislation concerning road vehicles, environmental health, health and safety at work, telecommunications, trading standards and retailing. The law in these areas is almost always enforced by non-police agencies. An observer might well, therefore, expect there to have been an increase in non-police prosecutions so that the answer of the largest group to question 8 is surprising. It is perhaps explicable partly by reference to the 32.4 per cent of justices' clerks who were undecided about whether there had been an increase; partly by the fact that many agencies prefer to enforce the law by warnings and encouragement wherever possible, using prosecution as a last resort; and partly by the fact that some of the agencies (with very limited resources) have ceased to being prosecutions in relation to certain offences in order to bring cases relating to newer provisions (or at least to be more selective in regard to which type of cases they bring).

Q9   Non-police Prosecutions are Decreasing Significantly

Thirty-one (45.6 per cent) magistrates disagreed. Seventeen (25 per cent) a little and 14 (20.6 per cent) strongly. Twenty-five (36.8 per cent) were undecided. Eleven (16.2 per cent) agreed a little with the statement and one agreed strongly.

The profile of opinion here seems to support the inference expressed (above) in relation to question 8, that the level of non-CPS prosecutions has remained fairly stable – despite an increase in law enforceable by the agencies – because those agencies have not enjoyed a increase in funding proportionate to their augmented responsibilities and are therefore having to be selective in the type of cases they prosecute. There is, as we have noted in chapter one, no central register from which we can judge the number of annual non-CPS prosecutions. As the table below shows, the has been a significant growth in recent times in the number of notifiable offences recorded by non-Home Office police forces, like the British Transport Police, from a total of 69,010 in 1996/7 to 79,300 in 1999/2000.

Table 4.1   Notifiable offences recorded by non-Home Office police forces

England and Wales		Number of offences		
Year	Total	British Transport Police	Ministry of Defence	UK Atomic Energy Authority
1996/1997	69,010	63,030	5,740	240
1997/1998	64,840	58,880	5,740	220
1998/1999	72,920	65,850	6,820	250
1999/2000	79,300	71,660	7,440	200

Source: Home Office Recorded Crime Statistics, 18 July 2000, ISSN 1358–510X, p. 13.

Q10   The Prosecutions Currently Undertaken by Non-police Agencies Would be Better Dealt with as Administrative Offences Outside the Criminal Justice System

Thirty-five (51.5 per cent) magistrates disagreed with the proposition – 25 (36.8 per cent) disagreed strongly and 10 (14.7 per cent) a little. Thirteen (19.1 per cent) agreed a little and six (8.8 per cent) agreed strongly. Twelve (17.6 per cent) were undecided. Two did not reply to the question.

Given the very wide range of non-CPS prosecuting agencies and the highly varied nature of the offences covered by this question many justices' clerks expressed reservations about generalising. In fact, in their written comments, 20 per cent of justices' clerks were explicit about the difficulty of generalising.

Among these remarks were those which said it was 'very difficult to generalise'; 'different prosecutors have different resources, skills, philosophies, and different legislative frameworks'; 'there is no single system of non-police prosecutions'; '... the vast range of private prosecutors who have different approaches to procedure and prosecution'.

Certainly the findings of the court study here show a remarkable diversity of prosecutions and practices. Although, from the base of all cases logged at all three courts – 9,689 – over 80 per cent of the non-police prosecutions were brought by just four agencies, the remaining 20 per cent of cases came from 18 other agencies.

Borough/County Councils generated 41.2 per cent (3,991 cases); the DT/DVLA brought 23.9 per cent (2,320 cases); the TVLEO accounted for 9.5 per cent (920 cases); and the DSS brought 5.4 per cent (527 cases).

The remaining 20 per cent of prosecutions ranked in order of number of defendants were brought by: *Vehicle Inspectorate* (535, 5.5 per cent); *London Buses* (427, 4.4 per cent); *SW Trains* (271, 2.8 per cent); *Inland Revenue* (210, 2.2 per cent); *Customs & Excise* (123, 1.3 per cent); *Education Welfare* (118, 1.2 per cent); *Environment Agency* 97, 1.0 per cent); *DTI* (37, 0.4 per cent); *Trading Standards* (33, 0.3 per cent); *RSPCA* (25, 0.3 per cent); *Electricity Supply Companies* (18, 0.2 per cent); *HSE* (15, 0.2 per cent); *British Waterways* (10, 0.1 per cent); *Cab Law Enforcement* (6, 0.1 per cent); *BT Security* (4 cases); *Dept of Health* (1 case); *Ministry of Agriculture* (1 case).

Clearly, many justices' clerks do not think that non-CPS prosecutions *in general* would be better dealt with as administrative offences outside the criminal justice system but some do have such a belief in respect of particular types of offence. Of the respondents, 17.6 per cent mentioned TV licence cases in particular as matters that should be dealt with outside of the criminal courts. This is perhaps an understandable view in light of the facts that, so many prosecutions are brought (with all that implies in terms of costs, resources and court time) and that the resultant convictions seem to cause more problems than they solve. Many of the defendants are people who are at the bottom of the social income league and who will therefore find it as difficult to pay a fine as to pay the licence fee. In the commenting on this, one justices' clerk said that these cases often involve 'single mothers on benefit unable to pay any fine'.

Certainly it is clear that TV licence cases occupy a great deal of the time of magistrates' courts. Samuels (1986) suggests that between one-fifth and one-quarter of all cases coming before the criminal courts are prosecutions by non- police agencies and individuals, almost entirely the former; and mostly relatively minor and in the magistrate's courts. He suggests (1986, p. 35) that the distribution of these cases is along the following lines (very approximately);

Television Licences	25%
Vehicle Excise Licence (tax disc)	18%
Transport	17%
Local Authority	11%
Retail stores	10%
Social Security fraud	7%
Customs and Excise VAT	3%
Individuals	2%

In the present writer's research, the Television Licence Enforcement Office (TVLEO) was, of 23 non-CPS prosecutors, the third most prolific bringer of cases: Across all three courts it brought 920 prosecutions amounting to 9.5 per cent of all cases in the sample.

General Comments

One justices' clerk who disagreed strongly with the proposition in question 10 commented that to have the matters currently dealt with as non-CPS prosecutions moved outside the criminal justice system 'would be a breach of "Human Rights" legislation'. This raises a very important point. It is true to say that someone who is faced with the accusation of a 'crime' is under Article 6(1) of the European Convention on Human Rights (and, thereby under the Human Rights Act 1998) entitled to a 'fair and public hearing'. The defendant must have the right (Art. 6(2)c) 'to defend himself in person or through legal assistance of his own choosing'. It would, therefore, amount to a violation of this legislation if a legal system permitted someone to be 'convicted' of the 'crime' of nonpayment of a TV licence in circumstances in which he or she did not have recourse to a trial. The answer to this from those who advocate the moving such matters into the administrative realm is to make them civil wrongs.

One magistrate commented:

> Justice must be seen to be done, and it is important that defendants have the opportunity to appear before a court to argue their case. I have seen tribunals at work on non-criminal work and I was surprised at the lack of knowledge of

evidential matters. I would however like to see television licence evasion decriminalised. If it is to remain an offence then magistrates courts are the appropriate forum for such hearings.

Further General Comments

If the overall level of enforcement increased significantly there would be initially a reaction from the public who would be unused to a highly proactive prosecuting policy. This is likely to be short lived as people would start complying with the law as the chances of prosecution increase.

Prosecutions of environmental offences are increasing but still in small numbers. Often these cases are investigated very thoroughly and presented well but there are so few of them that it is difficult to draw firm conclusions.

Non-police prosecutions cover a very wide range of offending – from unlicensed fishing to very serious health and safety cases. Degrees of efficiency on the part of the agencies also varies – local authorities and government departments being generally good.

The questions are not very well framed in regard to the marking system and I doubt any collation of the results of this questionnaire could produce meaningful conclusions. I'm sorry to be so blunt.

It is difficult to answer such general questions. Some non-police prosecuting authorities are very good, others are often poor. Those that employ or instruct qualified people tend to do better on the whole.

Chapter Five

Conclusions and Implications for Public Policy

The criminal justice system has recently been the subject of widespread heated debate in parliament, the broadcast media and the print media and in academic and professional journals.

The Official Home Office crime figures for England and Wales show that there were 5.3 million offences recorded by the police in the 12 months to March 2000, an increase of 3.8 per cent over the previous 12 month period (Home Office Statistical Bulletin, 18 July 2000, ISSN 1358–510X). None the less, as one recent Home Office publication explains: 'No one knows the true extent of crime in this or indeed any other country' (Information on the Criminal Justice System in England and Wales, Digest 4, October 1999, p. 1).

The British Crime Survey (BCS) (Home Office Statistical Bulletin, issue 21/98) estimates there were nearly 16,500,000 crimes against adults living in households in 1997. The long term trend shows that the gradual rise in BCS crime during the 1980s and the steeper rise during the early 1990s have now been reversed. Even so, the number of crimes counted by the BCS has increased by 49 per cent since 1981.

It is common now for lawyers, academics and commentators to refer to something called 'the criminal justice system'. This has been, for many years, an accepted descriptive term. Officially, however, there is no such thing as the 'criminal justice system'. Governmental responsibilities, for example, overlap in this area. The Home Secretary is responsible for the Metropolitan Police, criminal statistics, the Probation Service, and the Crown Prosecution Service (and, more broadly, for 'law and order'), while the Lord Chancellor is responsible for all the criminal law courts, the appointment of magistrates, and the judges. Nonetheless, in recent times, there has been increasing governmental recognition of something called the 'criminal justice system'. On 30 December 1998, for example, a single official statement entitled 'Joint Press Release on the Criminal Justice System Public Service Agreement' was issued on behalf of the Home Office, the Lord Chancellor's Department, and the Attorney General's Office. It stated:

> The overarching aims, objectives and performance measures for the criminal justice system have been published for the first time in a cross departmental Public Service Agreement. The three Departments, and their respective services, will be working more closely than ever before to ensure that the criminal justice system protects the public and delivers justice. Inter-agency cooperation will be promoted at regional, local, as well as at the national level. Ministers believe that these arrangements are a good example of 'joined-up government' in practice (http://www.nds.coi.gov.uk/coi/coipress.ns).

The significance of such a pronouncement is that it reveals an attempt to make coordinated policy in respect of each of these branches of operation. In fact, the statement goes on to become quite explicit:

> The three ministers have set two overarching aims to provide a strategic direction for the system as a whole. They have made clear that every part of the criminal justice system (including the police, courts, Crown Prosecution Service, prison and probation services) should work together so as to best serve and protect the public.
>
> The two overarching aims are:

- to reduce crime and the fear of crime and their social and economic costs; and
- to dispense justice fairly and efficiently and to promote confidence in the rule of law.

Supporting the aims are the following eight objectives:

in support of the first aim:
1)   to reduce the level of actual crime and disorder;
2)   to reduce the adverse impact of crime and disorder on people's lives;
3)   to reduce the economic costs of crime;

in support of the second aim:
4)   to ensure just processes and just and effective outcomes;
5)   to deal with cases throughout the criminal justice process with appropriate speed;
6)   to meet the needs of victims, witnesses and jurors within the system;
7)   to respect the rights of defendants and to treat them fairly;
8)   to promote confidence in the criminal justice system.

The criminal justice system costs over £12 billion a year to run. It is, therefore, a matter of singular importance in the formulation of public policy to ensure that any major working part of such a system is properly geared into the other working parts. The number of defendants prosecuted in 1997 was 1.86 million, and it is known that between 20 per cent and 25 per cent of prosecutions are brought by non-CPS agencies. This means that within the criminal justice system something in the order of 400,000 cases each year are being prosecuted by agencies other than the CPS. The non-CPS prosecutors are many and varied. Yet, even although they are all doing the same thing in prosecuting defendants in the criminal courts, they have no single coordinating body, do not share their work experiences in any way (e.g. by conference attendance, or through professional associations) and have very different outlooks and *modi operandi*.

In this research project, the work of 23 such agencies was examined but there are several other agencies whose work simply did not feature in the 1998 caseload for the three courts looked at in this study. The work of these other non-CPS bodies is not negligible. For example, the total number of crimes recorded by British Transport Police, Ministry of Defence police and UK Atomic Energy Authority police for 1999/2000 was 79,300.

One of the features of the territory of non-police prosecutions uncovered by the Royal Commission study (Lidstone et al., 1980) is the great variety inherent in the phenomenon. First, there is a variety of prosecutors – from large government departments, through local authorities, minor public authorities, special police forces, retail stores and voluntary societies to private individuals. Then there is a variety of functions as these different bodies use prosecution for very different purposes, to a very different extent, and in varying relationships to other enforcement measures. Additionally, there is a variety of prosecutorial arrangements, with access to legal advice on prosecution varying between agencies and regions and within different parts of a single agency. Another important aspect of variety in this field is the variety of ways of liaising with the police. In relation to some agencies the police were actively involved in investigating and assisting with prosecutions whereas in relation to other agencies they were not particularly cooperative.

The Royal Commission study (Lidstone et al., 1980, pp. 185–7) identified three ways in which policy might develop following publication of its report. In their first future scenario there is a growing tendency of the police, especially in the large urban areas where they feel most stretched, to leave as many cases as possible for agencies to prosecute. The second scenario concerns the possibility of massive increases in non police prosecutions as a result of changes in agency policy. It could be, they speculate, that in the future regulatory offences will be taken much more seriously by the state with a consequential growth in the number of prosecutions for such crime. The third possibility involves a government-led reduction in the number of prosecutions for such crime. That scenario also involves a government-led reduction in the number of different revenue collecting agencies. For example, vehicle excise licences could be abolished and the money collected through additional tax on petrol, and also the BBC could in future be financed through the taxation system and no longer through television licence fees.

The scenery has changed significantly in the 20 years since The Royal Commission study (Lidstone et al., 1980) wrote. Five years after publication of the Commission study, the Crown Prosecution Service was established eliminating the police as the prosecutors of ordinary crime. There has also been much privatisation in the areas of transport, the utilities and telecommunications. Before the establishment of the Crown Prosecution Service in 1985 the Royal Commission on Criminal Procedure (1979) issued a Consultative Paper which explored a number of possible options for reorganising the prosecution system in England and Wales. One of the options was a 'National Prosecution Agency' with control of prosecution policy at national level, and regional offices servicing police forces in their area – an option which was eventually adopted for the new CPS. It would have, of course, been possible to have also brought all non-police prosecutions within the ambit of this new service. The model existing in Scotland at that time and now is one based on a system that does include virtually all non-police prosecutions within the jurisdiction of the Scottish Procurator Fiscal although even in Scotland the British Transport Police, and educational authorities can prosecute separately. It is worth noting that in Scotland an official committee, the Thomson Committee, has recommended that all agency and similar prosecutions should in future be at the instance of the Procurator Fiscal, but this recommendation has not been taken up (Scottish Office, 1975, paras 31.05, 31.07). In advancing the idea of a single prosecution service the Royal Commission on Criminal Procedure for England and Wales identified the major arguments in favour of such a system as being (1979, para. 4):

> Greater uniformity of prosecution policy in general and more consistency as between decisions in individual cases; and greater accountability in the system both in relation to general policy and to particular cases.

Clearly, such arguments, in as much as they apply to all police prosecutions across the country, also apply to non-police prosecutions, particularly in view of the very many and highly varied types of prosecuting agency that exist today. As the Royal Commission study (Lidstone et al., 1980, p. 189) notes:

> The police are a body of public servants whose recommendations for prosecutions, the argument goes, should be more publicly accountable; if that is so it is hard to see why other public servants in public departments, local authorities, public utilities and the like, should not have their prosecutorial function similarly scrutinised.

There would, of course now, as then, be enormous difficulties in shifting this burden of work to a central prosecuting agency. Any such supra-agency would, in effect, without its own establishment of experts second guessing or duplicating the work of any individual agency's staff be wholly reliant on the work and decisions of an agency like the HSE or the RSPCA. The problem of insufficient knowledge and expertise in relation to particular types of prosecution is aggravated by the fact that many specialist types of prosecution are much more common in one geographic region than another, for example the paucity or absence of Customs and Excise prosecutions in many areas.

Moreover, many organisations like the HSE operate on the basis of a delicate mix of advisory, educational, persuasive, and law enforcement modes – a balance which would arguably be seriously disturbed if the decision as to whether to prosecute were being taken by an external public prosecutor. In recommending the extension of the Procurator Fiscal's jurisdiction to include all agency prosecutions, the Thomson Committee said: 'In deciding whether or not to prosecute, the Procurator Fiscal would exercise his discretion on the same uniform basis as he applies to all other cases …'(Scottish Office, 1975, p. 122). There would, however, be serious difficulties were such an option ever to be adopted because a Procurator Fiscal or public prosecutor would then have to try to establish a uniformity that may not create justice in all cases. If prosecuting across all cases on the 'same uniform basis' simply means that the prosecutor must be satisfied that all cases brought by the police or any agency were only taken forward on legally and evidentially sound grounds then clearly a uniformity could be achieved. But it would not be a substantive uniformity.

> A prosecutor seriously interested in substantive uniformity would be obliged, for example, to ask the Inland Revenue whether it was really just to prosecute the few most serious in each different *category* of case, when this meant prosecuting for some trifling frauds and reaching settlements with other for frauds of many thousands of pounds (Lidstone et al., 1980, p. 191).

In Scotland where the Factory Inspectorate has been obliged, since 1974, to send all the cases that it wishes to prosecute through the Procurator Fiscal's office, there have been some highly problematic cases. These have occurred where the inspectorate, which uses its prosecution power as a last resort, has resolved to prosecute in a case only to have this wish thwarted by the Procurator Fiscal's office (Lidstone et al., 1980, p. 191).

Another difficulty here concerns the political balance between the executive and the judiciary. The extent to which various agencies decide to use prosecution as a primary tool of enforcement is, under the current arrangements, subject to a considerable degree of social and political consideration. Thus crack downs on social security fraud through a more ready recourse to prosecution were orchestrated through governmental pressure in the early 1980s and again at the turn of the century. A system in which prosecutorial discretion was much more controlled by central public prosecution agency would be able to resist such governmental pressure to increase or slacken the use of prosecutions by a particular agency, and thus galvanise a major dispute about the proper allocation of such decision-making within the established model of the separation of powers.

Another great difficulty with instituting a system of public prosecution for all non-police cases is that the organisational regional boundaries of many of the non-police agencies like the utility companies and the Health and Safety Executive, are not coterminous with those of the relevant police (and now CPS) boundaries. This means that there would be enormous difficulties for the various agencies (which would be gathering evidence for, and preparing prosecutions) in liaising with the different prosecution districts.

This research project generated a great quantity of data, many parts of which have been presented and digested earlier in this text. Here, in conclusion, I identify some of those data which have implications for policy and strategic development of systems and processes within the criminal justice system.

1) Of the 9,689 cases in the study, 80 per cent were brought by just four of the 23 agencies that prosecuted cases in the magistrates courts, with Borough and County councils prosecuting 41.2 per cent (3,989) of all cases.
2) In these council prosecutions no appearance of the defendant was registered in 55.7 per cent of cases, and 69.1 per cent of defendants were found guilty.
3) Considering all 9,689 cases within the study, no appearance of the defendant was recorded in 4,845 (49.6 per cent) of cases.

4) Considering all 9,689 cases, defendants were convicted in 6,555 (67.7 per cent) of cases.
5) In cases where there was a conviction, 93.8 per cent of defendants were given a fine, and 0.2 per cent (14) were given a custodial sentence.
6) There are wide differences of prosecutorial policy in the different areas. For example, of the 2,320 cases prosecuted by the Department of Transport and DVLA, 80 per cent were brought in Milton Keynes, with 19 per cent of cases being brought at Newcastle-under-Lyme and only 1 per cent at Horseferry Road in London. Similarly, of the 118 defendants prosecuted under the 1996 Education Act for failure to ensure a child attends school regularly, 78 per cent of prosecutions were at Milton Keynes. Of the 97 cases brought by the Environment Agency, 89 per cent (87 cases) were brought at Newcastle-under-Lyme.
7) Of those that were found guilty across all courts and for all offences, 96 per cent had pleaded guilty. These cases are, therefore, arguably not really legal fights of the sort that are typical in the mainstream of the criminal justice system.
8) Of those that were found guilty the largest proportion were those that 'did not appear in court' (55 per cent).
9) The agencies have remarkably different rates of success. The Inland Revenue enjoyed a 99 per cent success rate, contrasted with success rates of under 35 per cent from other agencies.
10) Only 203 defendants (2.1 per cent) were represented in court.

The more information that was gathered and recorded for this study, the more that it became evident just how little is really known about such an expansive and important part of the criminal justice system. Prosecutions by organisations other than the Crown Prosecution Service are many, varied and high consequential in social terms. They cost a lot and they affect millions of lives. Yet, they are not categorised together as a system and they are not the subject of any central registration of data not training nor public spending. The evidence suggests that there is a great deal of further research to be conducted in this area, and it is hoped that this study has gone some way towards: a) exposing the areas in which it would be profitable to acquire knowledge; and b) raising some questions about law and policy that might be addressed in other projects.

APPENDICES

Appendix 1

This appendix presents summaries of the purpose and structure of the different organisations (within this study) exercising a prosecutorial role in the magistrates' courts.

Driver and Vehicle Licensing Agency

The primary responsibilities of the Driver and Vehicle Licensing Agency (DVLA) are the licensing of drivers in Great Britain, the registration and licensing of vehicles and the collection and enforcement of vehicle excise duty (VED) in the UK. This involves the collection of over £4.7 billion a year in VED and the maintenance of 38 million driver records and 27 million licensed vehicle records. The DVLA provides a wide range of services to the motoring public, the motor industry, the police, the courts, and other governmental departments. The full cost of the Agency's operations is around £200 million a year. The Agency is an executive branch of the Department of the Environment, Transport of the Regions (DETR).

Vehicle Inspectorate

The Vehicle Inspectorate is also an agency of the DETR (above). Its objective is to improve road safety and environmental standards. Its main task, carried out in cooperation with other enforcement agencies such as the police and local authority trading standards officers, is to ensure that motor vehicles are maintained to minimum standards laid down by law. Activities include: supervising the MOT scheme; conducting statutory testing of lorries, coaches and buses; carrying out roadside checks and other spot checks on vehicles; advising Traffic Commissioners in their licensing function; undertaking specialised inspections; investigating accidents and defects; and overseeing recall campaigns. The Vehicle Inspectorate is a trading fund, recovering its costs through charges. It has headquarters in Bristol and employs over 1,600 staff. Its running costs are approximately £64 million per year.

Trading Standards Authorities

These authorities throughout the UK are local government law enforcement agencies. They enforce consumer related criminal legislation, as well as being providers of advice and assistance to the UK's consumers and businesses. These authorities have four main areas of responsibility: fair trading, safety, metrology (weights and measures) and quality standards. Fair trading relates to trades descriptions, consumer credit, and prices. Safety relates to consumer protection, product safety, and petroleum. Metrology relates to all weights and measures regulations. Quality standards relate to fertilisers, feedingstuffs, pesticides, and the environment. Fair Trading legislation such as the Trade Descriptions Act 1968, the Fair Trading Act 1973, the Consumer Credit Act 1974, and the Consumer Protection Act 1987, has been the major growth area for the trading standards service since the late 1960s, with an enormous added responsibility for ensuring 'truthfulness in trade'. Trading Standards Authorities also prosecute in cases involving the Sale of Goods Act 1979, the Trading Schemes Act 1996, the Price Marking Order 1991, the Copyright Designs and Patents Act 1988, the Timeshare Act 1992, the Property Misdescriptions Act 1991 and the Video Recordings Acts of 1984 and 1993.

The Inland Revenue

The Revenue is responsible for the administration of income tax, capital gains tax, corporation tax, petroleum revenue tax, inheritance tax and stamp duty and from 1 April 1999 it merged with the Contributions Agency (CA). The CA, which was responsible for National Insurance Contributions (NIC), after the merger became, in part, the National Insurance Contributions Office (NICO). The Inland Revenue is also responsible for the collection of student loan repayments.

HM Customs & Excise

This Agency has a wide range of responsibilities from collecting VAT and Excise Duties to safeguarding endangered species. It brings in around 40 per cent of central government's total taxation yield, and has a policing role in respect of illegal drugs, firearms and paedophile material. In the 1997/98 financial year Customs & Excise collected over £50 billion in VAT receipts, and over £35.5 billion in Excise Duties. In the same year, the Department seized more than £3.3 billion worth of drugs, 200 illicit importations of firearms and explosives, and almost 3,000 endangered live animals and birds.

TV Licensing

TV Licensing is a trading name used by Envision Licensing Limited. Over 1,200 staff are employed at the Contract Centre in Bristol and over 500 throughout the UK. The Broadcasting Act 1990 made the BBC responsible for licence administration and TV licensing is contracted to the BBC. The role of TV Licensing is to send out reminders, process queries, applications and payments, and to use its Enforcement Office (EO) to prosecute people who are using a TV without a licence.

Health and Safety Executive

The Health and Safety Executive (HSE) is the executive branch of the Health and Safety Commission whose mission is to ensure that risks to people's health and safety from work activities are properly controlled. It undertakes prosecutions under the Health And Safety At Work etc. Act 1974. The HSE/S employ about 3,900 staff.

The Royal Society for the Prevention of Cruelty to Animals (RSPCA)

The Animal Protection Act 1822, sponsored by the MP Richard Martin, which outlawed cruelty to cattle, horses and sheep, was the world's first anti-cruelty law. Two years later the SPCA was founded and backed by four MPs, and received permission in 1840 from Queen Victoria to describe itself as the Royal Society for the Prevention of Cruelty to Animals. Today the RSPCA has 309 inspectors investigating over 100,000 cruelty complaints a year in England and Wales.

British Waterways

British Waterways (BW) has as its primary responsibility ensuring that British canals and rivers are safe for people to enjoy. It is also concerned with looking after the wider waterway environment; the buildings and wildlife associated with canals and rivers. It is responsible to the DETR (above). Half the population of Britain lives within five miles of part of the waterway network.

The Ministry of Agriculture, Fisheries and Food

The Ministry of Agriculture, Fisheries and Food (MAFF) has the aim to ensure that consumers benefit from competitively priced food, produced to high standards of safety. It also aims to ensure that consumers benefit from environmental care and animal safety and from a sustainable, efficient food chain. Among its objectives is one to protect public health in relation to food and to animal diseases transmissible to humans.

The Department of Social Security

The Department of Social Security (DSS) operates a Benefit Fraud Inspectorate (BFI), an independent unit set up to inspect social security benefits administration and counter-fraud activity within DSS agencies and local authorities. The DSS prosecutes in cases of alleged fraud.

The Department of Trade and Industry

The Department of Trade and Industry (DTI) is the primary government agency for coordination, promotion and facilitation activities relating to trade, industry and investments. It acts as a catalyst for intensified private sector activity to accelerate and sustain economic growth. The Department aims for investment expansion, export growth, countryside development and improvement and protection of consumer welfare. It prosecutes in cases where there is evidence that companies have violated the law in relation to any of the foregoing areas.

The Environment Agency

The Environment Agency reports to the DETR. It operates from seven regional offices in England and one in Cardiff representing Environment Agency Wales. It employs 9,500 staff. The EA has a wide range of responsibilities including the quality of air, land and water; pollution control and river basin management; standards of waste disposal and the management of water resources.

London Underground

London Underground through regular ticket surveys and mathematical models estimate that each year a total of about £25 million is lost through all types of ticketless travel and fare evasion. The most common type of irregularity is travelling on the system without a ticket or an invalid ticket. The London Regional Transport (Penalty Fares) Act 1992 enabled £10 penalty fares to be introduced across London Underground. Passengers are liable for a penalty fare if found to be travelling on the system without a valid ticket, unless they were genuinely unable to obtain a ticket at the start of the journey. Many cases are dealt with in this way but London Underground continues to resort to other legal means such as its Bylaws and the Regulation of Railways Act 1989 when there is evidence of intent to travel fraudulently. London Underground also has the power to report deliberate fare evaders to the British Transport Police for possible prosecution in the courts. In 1998 there were a total of 24,817 reported cases of suspected fare evasion on LU. There were 5,216 prosecutions for fare evasion, with another 19,601 cases dealt with by other means, usually a caution and payment made.

London Transport Buses

There are about 5,400 buses running on the 700 routes in the London Transport Buses system. The number of journeys on LT bus services in 1998–99 was 1,267 million which is around 4 million journeys a day on a typical weekday, compared with 2.5 million on the London Underground. Fare evasion and other ticket irregularities on London's buses cost London Transport Buses an estimated £21 million a year. LT Buses carries private prosecutions of alleged offenders who on conviction could face a maximum penalty of £1,000.

The Education Welfare Service

Education welfare services are operated out of local authorities. Part of the function of Education Welfare Services is to provide a comprehensive support to promote and maintain good school attendance. The local authority, through the Education Welfare Service, will prosecute in cases of sustained non-attendance at school. The 1944 Education Act lays upon the parent the duty to see that the child of compulsory school age (5–16) receives full time education suitable to his age, ability and aptitude either by regular attendance at school or otherwise. The responsibility for ensuring that the parent carries out his duty lies with the Local Education Authority. Failure by a parent to fulfil his statutory duty can result in the issuing by the Authority of a School Attendance Order. It is when these have been violated that prosecutions can follow. In addition to the parents' duty to ensure that their child receives an efficient full time education, parents also have a duty to see that their child regularly attends the school at which he is a registered pupil. If the child fails to attend regularly the parent could be guilty of an offence.

Appendix 2

P1   Prosecutor and plea

Absolute analysis %
Break %

Respondents	Base	Guilty	Not guilty	Guilty MCA	Not guilty MCA	No appearance	Not known	N/A
				What was the plea?				
	9,688	1,301	329	1,247	54	4,806	1,593	359
		13.4%	3.4%	12.9%	0.6%	49.6%	16.4%	3.7%
Who was the prosecutor?								
DT/DVLA	2,320	183	36	464	10	1,432	106	89
	23.9%	7.9%	1.6%	20.0%	0.4%	61.7%	4.6%	3.8%
		14.1%	10.9%	37.2%	18.5%	29.8%	6.7%	24.8%
Vehicle Inspectorate	535	99	14	239	28	83	71	1
	5.5%	18.5%	2.6%	44.7%	5.2%	15.5%	13.3%	0.2%
		7.6%	4.3%	19.2%	51.9%	1.7%	4.5%	0.3%
TVLEO	920	67	13	136	3	491	192	18
	9.5%	7.3%	1.4%	14.8%	0.3%	53.4%	20.9%	2.0%
		5.1%	4.0%	10.9%	5.6%	10.2%	12.1%	5.0%
Environment Agency	97	6	0.0%	37	0.0%	34	16	4
	1.0%	6.2%	0.0%	38.1%	0.0%	35.1%	16.5%	4.1%
		0.5%		3.0%		0.7%	1.0%	1.1%
Electricity	18	0.0%	0.0%	0.0%	0.0%	10	8	0.0%
	0.2%	0.0%	0.0%	0.0%	0.0%	55.6%	44.4%	0.0%
						0.2%	0.5%	
DSS	527	233	33	0.0%	0.0%	60	195	6
	5.4%	44.2%	6.3%	0.0%	0.0%	11.4%	37.0%	1.1%
		17.9%	10.0%			1.2%	12.2%	1.7%
RSPCA	25	7	5	0.0%	0.0%	9	4	0.0%
	0.3%	28.0%	20.0%	0.0%	0.0%	36.0%	16.0%	0.0%
		0.5%	1.5%			0.2%	0.3%	
DTI	37	4	2	0.0%	0.0%	7	23	1
	0.4%	10.8%	5.4%	0.0%	0.0%	18.9%	62.2%	2.7%
		0.3%	0.6%			0.1%	1.4%	0.3%
Trading Standards	33	11	13	0.0%	6	1	2	0.0%
	0.3%	33.3%	39.4%	0.0%	18.2%	3.0%	6.1%	0.0%
		0.8%	4.0%		11.1%	0.0%	0.1%	
Education Welfare	118	49	2	4	0.0%	43	20	0.0%
	1.2%	41.5%	1.7%	3.4%	0.0%	36.4%	16.9%	0.0%
		3.8%	0.6%	0.3%		0.9%	1.3%	
British Waterways	10	1	0.0%	5	0.0%	4	0.0%	0.0%
	0.1%	10.0%	0.0%	50.0%	0.0%	40.0%	0.0%	0.0%
		0.1%		0.4%		0.1%		
BT Security	4	1	0.0%	0.0%	0.0%	2	1	0.0%
	0.0%	25.0%	0.0%	0.0%	0.0%	50.0%	25.0%	0.0%
		0.1%				0.0%	0.1%	
Inland Revenue	210	1	0.0%	0.0%	0.0%	206	3	0.0%
	2.2%	0.5%	0.0%	0.0%	0.0%	98.1%	1.4%	0.0%
		0.1%				4.3%	0.2%	

Customs & Excise	123	31	14	0.0%	0.0%	12	65	1
	1.3%	25.2%	11.4%	0.0%	0.0%	9.8%	52.8%	0.8%
		2.4%	4.3%			0.2%	4.1%	0.3%
HSE	15	5	0.0%	0.0%	0.0%	2	8	0.0%
	0.2%	33.3%	0.0%	0.0%	0.0%	13.3%	53.5%	0.0%
		0.4%				0.0%	0.5%	
SW Trains	271	87	17	0.0%	0.0%	78	79	10
	2.8%	32.1%	6.3%	0.0%	0.0%	28.8%	29.2%	3.7%
		6.7%	5.2%			1.6%	5.0%	2.8%
Cab Law Enforcement	6	5	1	0.0%	0.0%	0.0%	0.0%	0.0%
	0.1%	83.3%	16.7%	0.0%	0.0%	0.0%	0.0%	0.0%
		0.4%	0.3%					
London Buses	427	113	23	0.0%	1	110	155	25
	4.4%	26.5%	5.4%	0.0%	0.2%	25.8%	36.3%	5.9%
		8.7%	7.0%		1.0%	2.3%	9.7%	7.0%
Dept. of Health	1	0.0%	1	0.0%	0.0%	0.0%	0.0%	0.0%
	0.0%	0.0%	100.0%	0.0%	0.0%	0.0%	0.0%	0.0%
			0.3%					
Borough/County Councils	3,990	397	155	362	6	2,221	645	204
	41.2%	9.9%	3.9%	9.1%	0.2%	55.7%	16.2%	5.1%
		30.5%	47.1%	29.0%	11.1%	46.2%	40.5%	56.8%
Ministry of Agriculture	1	1	0.0%	0.0%	0.0%	0.0%	0.0%	0.0%
	0.0%	100.0%	0.0%	0.0%	0.0%	0.0%	0.0%	0.0%
		0.1%						

P2   Prosecutor and verdict

Absolute analysis %
Break %

Each cell below shows: count / break % (row) / absolute % (column). Where the count is zero only the percentages (0.0% / 0.0%) are shown.

	Base	Verdict							
		Not guilty	Withdrawn/ dismissed	Adjourned	Warrant issued for	Summons not served	Remanded in custody	Remanded on bail	Emergency probation order
Respondents	**9,688**	**6** / **0.1%**	**1,047** / **10.8%**	**1,343** / **13.9%**	**47** / **0.5%**	**358** / **3.7%**	**81** / **0.8%**	**251** / **2.6%**	**0.0%**
Who was the prosecutor?									
DT/DVLA	2,320 / 23.9%	0.0% / 0.0%	210 / 9.1% / 20.1%	162 / 7.0% / 12.1%	1 / 0.0% / 2.1%	93 / 4.0% / 28.0%	0.0% / 0.0%	1 / 0.0% / 0.4%	0.0% / 0.0%
Vehicle Inspectorate	535 / 5.5%	1 / 0.2% / 10.7%	26 / 4.9% / 2.5%	139 / 26.0% / 10.3%	0.0% / 0.0%	1 / 0.2% / 0.3%	0.0% / 0.0%	8 / 1.5% / 3.2%	0.0% / 0.0%
TVLEO	920 / 9.5%	0.0% / 0.0%	165 / 17.9% / 15.8%	83 / 9.0% / 6.2%	0.0% / 0.0%	18 / 2.0% / 5.0%	0.0% / 0.0%	0.0% / 0.0%	0.0% / 0.0%
Environment Agency	97 / 1.0%	0.0% / 0.0%	13 / 13.4% / 1.2%	6 / 6.2% / 0.4%	0.0% / 0.0%	6 / 6.2% / 1.7%	0.0% / 0.0%	0.0% / 0.0%	0.0% / 0.0%
Electricity	16 / 0.2%	0.0% / 0.0%	2 / 11.1% / 0.2%	9 / 50.0% / 0.7%	0.0% / 0.0%	0.0% / 0.0%	0.0% / 0.0%	2 / 11.1% / 0.8%	0.0% / 0.0%
DSS	527 / 5.4%	1 / 0.2% / 16.7%	11 / 2.1% / 1.1%	76 / 14.4% / 5.7%	33 / 8.3% / 70.2%	5 / 0.9% / 1.4%	0.0% / 0.0%	184 / 34.9% / 73.3%	0.0% / 0.0%
RSPCA	25 / 0.3%	0.0% / 0.0%	1 / 4.0% / 0.1%	9 / 36.0% / 0.7%	2 / 8.0% / 4.3%	0.0% / 0.0%	0.0% / 0.0%	6 / 24.0% / 2.4%	0.0% / 0.0%
DTI	37 / 0.4%	0.0% / 0.0%	5 / 13.5% / 0.5%	15 / 40.5% / 1.1%	1 / 2.7% / 2.1%	1 / 2.7% / 0.3%	0.0% / 0.0%	10 / 27.0% / 4.0%	0.0% / 0.0%
Trading Standards	33 / 0.3%	0.0% / 0.0%	2 / 6.1% / 0.2%	5 / 15.2% / 0.4%	0.0% / 0.0%	0.0% / 0.0%	0.0% / 0.0%	8 / 24.2% / 3.2%	0.0% / 0.0%

Education Welfare	118 / 1.2%	0.0% 0.0%	4 / 3.4% / 0.4%	35 / 29.7% / 2.6%	0.0% 0.0%	0.0% 0.0%	0.0% 0.0%	2 / 1.7% / 0.8%	0.0% 0.0%
British Waterways	10 / 0.1%	0.0% 0.0%	1 / 10.0% / 0.1%	0.0% 0.0%	0.0% 0.0%	0.0% 0.0%	0.0% 0.0%	0.0% 0.0%	0.0% 0.0%
BT Security	4 / 0.0%	0.0% 0.0%	0.0% 0.0%	1 / 25.0% / 0.1%	0.0% 0.0%	0.0% 0.0%	0.0% 0.0%	0.0% 0.0%	0.0% 0.0%
Inland Revenue	210 / 2.25	0.0% 0.0%	87 / 41.4% / 8.3%	120 / 57.1% / 8.9%	0.0% 0.0%	0.0% 0.0%	0.0% 0.0%	0.0% 0.0%	0.0% 0.0%
Customs & Excise	123 / 1.3%	0.0% 0.0%	4 / 3.3% / 0.4%	10 / 8.1% / 0.7%	0.0% 0.0%	1 / 0.8% / 0.3%	76 / 61.8% / 93.8%	17 / 13.8% / 6.8%	0.0% 0.0%
HSE	15 / 0.2%	0.0% 0.0%	0.0% 0.0%	8 / 53.3% / 0.6%	0.0% 0.0%	0.0% 0.0%	0.0% 0.0%	0.0% 0.0%	0.0% 0.0%
SW Trans	271 / 2.8%	0.0% 0.0%	24 / 8.9% / 2.3%	47 / 17.3% / 3.5%	1 / 0.4% / 2.1%	10 / 3.7% / 2.8%	0.0% 0.0%	0.0% 0.0%	0.0% 0.0%
Cab Law Enforcement	6 / 0.1%	0.0% 0.0%	1 / 16.7% / 0.1%	0.0% 0.0%	0.0% 0.0%	0.0% 0.0%	0.0% 0.0%	0.0% 0.0%	0.0% 0.0%
London Buses	427 / 4.4%	0.0% 0.0%	44 / 10.3% / 4.2%	56 / 13.1% / 2.1%	1 / 0.2% / 7.0%	25 / 15.9% / 1.2%	1 / 0.2% / 0.4%	1 / 0.2%	0.0% 0.0%
Dept. of Health	1 / 0.0%	0.0% 0.0%	0.0% 0.0%	1 / 100.0% / 0.1%	0.0% 0.0%	0.0% 0.0%	0.0% 0.0%	0.0% 0.0%	0.0% 0.0%
Borough/County Councils	3,990 / 41.2%	4 / 0.1% / 56.7%	447 / 11.2% / 42.7%	51 / 14.1% / 41.8%	8 / 0.2% / 17.0%	198 / 5.0% / 55.3%	4 / 0.1% / 4.9%	11 / 0.3% / 4.4%	0.0% 0.0%
Ministry of Agriculture	1 / 0.0%	0.0% 0.0%	0.0% 0.0%	0.0% 0.0%	0.0% 0.0%	0.0% 0.0% / 0.4%	0.0% 0.0%	1 / 100.0%	0.0% 0.0%

P3   Prosecutor and disposal

Absolute analysis %
Break %

Respondents	Base	Remanded on bail	Remanded in custody	If convicted what was the disposal?						
				Imprison-ment	Probation	Community Service	Combination Order	Absolute discharge	Conditional discharge	Sentence suspended
	6,554	126 / 1.9%	5 / 0.1%	14 / 0.2%	22 / 0.3%	56 / 0.9%	8 / 0.1%	80 / 1.2%	95 / 1.4	2 / 0.0%
Who was the prosecutor?										
DT/DVLA	1,853 / 28.3%	15 / 0.8% / 11.9%	0.0% / 0.0%	1 / 0.1% / 7.1%	0.0% / 0.0%	0.0% / 0.0%	0.0% / 0.0%	21 / 1.1% / 26.3%	2 / 0.1% / 2.1%	0.0% / 0.0%
Vehicle Inspectorate	360 / 5.5%	3 / 0.8% / 2.4%	0.0% / 0.0%	0.0% / 0.0%	0.0% / 0.0%	0.0% / 0.0%	0.0% / 0.0%	14 / 3.9% / 17.5%	0.0% / 0.0%	0.0% / 0.0%
TVLEO	654 / 10.0%	6 / 0.9% / 4.8%	0.0% / 0.0%	0.0% / 0.0%	0.0% / 0.0%	0.0% / 0.0%	0.0% / 0.0%	2 / 0.3% / 2.5%	3 / 0.5% / 3.2%	0.0% / 0.0%
Environmental Agency	72 / 1.1%	2 / 2.8%	0.0% / 0.0%	0.0% / 0.0%	1 / 1.4% / 4.5%	0.0% / 0.0%	0.0% / 0.0%	0.0% / 0.0%	0.0% / 0.0%	0.0% / 0.0%
Electricity	5 / 0.1%	5 / 100.0% / 4.0%	0.0% / 0.0%	0.0% / 0.0%	0.0% / 0.0%	0.0% / 0.0%	0.0% / 0.0%	0.0% / 0.0%	0.0% / 0.0%	0.0% / 0.0%
DSS	217 / 3.3%	69 / 31.8% / 54.8%	5 / 2.3% / 100.0%	9 / 4.1% / 64.3%	14 / 6.5% / 63.6%	52 / 24.0% / 92.9%	8 / 3.7% / 100.0%	0.0% / 0.0%	27 / 12.4% / 28.4%	1 / 0.5% / 50.0%
RSPCA	7 / 0.1%	0.0% / 0.0%	0.0% / 0.0%	1 / 14.3% / 7.1%	0.0% / 0.0%	0.0% / 0.0%	0.0% / 0.0%	0.0% / 0.0%	0.0% / 0.0%	0.0% / 0.0%
DTI	5 / 0.1%	0.0% / 0.0%	0.0% / 0.0%	0.0% / 0.0%	0.0% / 0.0%	1 / 20.0% / 1.6%	0.0% / 0.0%	0.0% / 0.0%	2 / 40.0% / 2.1%	1 / 20.0% / 50.0%
Trading Standards	18 / 0.3%	7 / 38.9% / 5.6%	0.0% / 0.0%	0.0% / 0.0%	0.0% / 0.0%	0.0% / 0.0%	0.0% / 0.0%	0.0% / 0.0%	4 / 22.2% / 4.2%	0.0% / 0.0%

Agency	C1	C2	C3	C4	C5	C6	C7	C8	C9	C10
Education Welfare	77 / 1.2%	5 / 6.5%	0.0%	0.0%	7 / 9.1%	0.0%	0.0%	3 / 3.9%	28 / 33.8%	0.0% / 0.0%
British Waterways	9 / 0.1%	4.0%	0.0%	0.0%	31.0%	0.0%	0.0%	3.8%	27.4%	0.0% / 0.0%
BT Security	3 / 0.0%	1 / 33.3%	0.0%	0.0%	0.0%	0.0%	0.0%	0.0%	1 / 33.3%	0.0% / 0.0%
Inland Revenue	2 / 0.0%	0.0%	0.0%	0.0%	0.0%	0.0%	0.0%	0.0%	0.0%	0.0% / 0.0%
Customs and Excise	15 / 0.2%	1 / 6.7% / 0.8%	0.0%	2 / 13.3% / 14.3%	0.0%	1 / 6.7% / 1.8%	0.0%	0.0%	2 / 13.3% / 2.1%	0.0% / 0.0%
HSE	7 / 0.1%	1 / 14.3% / 0.8%	0.0%	0.0%	0.0%	0.0%	0.0%	0.0%	0.0%	0.0% / 0.0%
SW Trains	189 / 2.9%	0.0%	0.0%	0.0%	0.0%	0.0%	0.0%	0.0%	2 / 1.1% / 2.1%	0.0% / 0.0%
Cab Law Enforcement	5 / 0.1%	0.0%	0.0%	0.0%	0.0%	0.0%	0.0%	0.0%	0.0%	0.0% / 0.0%
London Buses	299 / 4.6%	0.0%	0.0%	0.0%	0.0%	0.0%	0.0%	5 / 1.7% / 6.3%	2 / 0.7% / 2.1%	0.0% / 0.0%
Department of Health	0.0% / 0.0%	0.0%	0.0%	0.0%	0.0%	0.0%	0.0%	0.0%	0.0%	0.0% / 0.0%
Borough/County Councils	2,757 / 42.1%	11 / 0.4% / 8.7%	0.0%	1 / 0.0% / 7.1%	0.0%	2 / 0.1% / 3.6%	0.0%	35 / 1.3% / 43.8%	24 / 0.9% / 25.3%	0.0% / 0.0%
Ministry of Agriculture	0.0% / 0.0%	0.0%	0.0%	0.0%	0.0%	0.0%	0.0%	0.0%	0.0%	0.0% / 0.0%

P4   Prosecutor and accused's presence

Absolute analysis % Break % Respondents	Base	Was the 'accused' present in court?			
		Yes	No	Not known	N/A
	9,688	640	6,232	2,475	341
		6.6%	64.3%	25.5%	3.5%
Who was the prosecutor?					
DT/DVLA	2,320	70	1,930	227	93
	23.9%	3.0%	83.2%	9.8%	4.0%
		10.9%	31.0%	9.2%	27.3%
Vehicle Inspectorate	535	48	391	94	2
	5.5%	9.0%	73.1%	17.6%	0.4%
		7.5%	6.3%	3.8%	0.6%
TVLEO	920	10	632	269	18
	9.5%	1.1%	68.7%	28.3%	2.0%
		1.6%	10.1%	10.5%	5.3%
Environment Agency	97	4	76	11	6
	1.0%	4.1%	78.4%	11.3%	6.3%
		0.6%	1.2%	0.4%	1.8%
Electricity	18	2	10	6	0.0%
	0.2%	11.1%	55.6%	33.3%	0.0%
		0.3%	0.2%	0.2%	
DSS	527	227	73	221	6
	5.4%	43.1%	13.9%	41.9%	1.1%
		35.5%	1.2%	8.9%	1.8%
RSPCA	25	6	9	10	0.0%
	0.3%	24.0%	36.0%	40.0%	0.0%
		0.9%	0.1%	0.4%	
DTI	37	6	7	23	1
	0.4%	16.2%	18.9%	62.2%	2.7%
		0.9%	0.1%	0.9%	0.3%
Trading Standards	33	25	6	2	0.0%
	0.3%	75.8%	18.2%	6.1%	0.0%
		3.9%	0.1%	0.1%	
Education Welfare	118	28	50	40	0.0%
	1.2%	23.7%	42.4%	33.9%	0.0%
		4.4%	0.8%	1.6%	
British Waterways	10	0.0%	9	1	0.0%
	0.1%	0.0%	90.0%	10.0%	0.0%
			0.1%	0.0%	
BT Security	4	1	2	1	0.0%
	0.0%	25.0%	50.0%	25.0%	0.0%
		0.2%	0.0%	0.0%	
Inland Revenue	210	3	204	3	0.0%
	2.2%	1.4%	97.1%	1.4%	0.0%
		0.5%	3.3%	0.1%	
Customs & Excise	123	81	12	30	0.0%
	1.3%	65.9%	9.8%	24.4%	0.0%
		12.7%	0.2%	1.2%	
HSE	15	3	5	7	0.0%
	0.2%	20.0%	33.3%	46.7%	0.0%
		0.5%	0.1%	0.3%	

SW Trains	271	7	75	180	9
	2.8%	2.6%	27.7%	66.4%	3.3%
		1.1%	1.2%	7.3%	2.6%
Cab Law Enforcement	6	1	0.0%	5	0.0%
	0.1%	16.7%	0.0%	83.3%	0.0%
		0.2%		0.2%	
London Buses	427	11	113	278	25
	4.4%	2.6%	26.5%	65.1%	5.9%
		1.7%	1.8%	11.2%	7.3%
Dept. of Health	1	1	0.0%	0.0%	0.0%
	0.0%	100.0%	0.0%	0.0%	0.0%
		0.2%			
Borough/County	3,990	105,	2,627	1,076	181
Councils	41.2%	2.6%	65.9%	27.0%	4.5%
		16.4%	42.4%	43.5%	53.1%
Ministry of	1	1	0.0%	0.0%	0.0%
Agriculture	0.0%	100.0%	0.0%	0.0%	0.0%
		0.2%			

P5　　Prosecutor and represented defendants

Absolute analysis % Break % Respondents	Base	Yes	No	Not known	N/A
	9,687	203	1,729	7,410	345
		2.1%	17.8%	76.5%	3.6%
Who was the prosecutor?					
DT/DVLA	2,320	8	714	1,505	93
	23.9%	0.3%	30.8%	64.9%	4.0%
		3.9%	41.3%	20.3%	27.0%
Vehicle Inspectorate	535	52	327	154	2
	5.5%	9.7%	61.1%	28.8%	0.4%
		25.6%	18.9%	2.1%	0.6%
TVLEO	920	0.0%	200	702	18
	9.5%	0.0%	21.7%	76.3%	2.0%
			11.6%	9.5%	5.2%
Environment Agency	97	0.0%	74	17	6
	1.0%	0.0%	76.3%	17.5%	6.2%
			4.3%	0.2%	1.7%
Electricity	18	7	5	6	0.0%
	0.2%	38.9%	27.8%	33.3%	0.0%
		3.4%	0.3%	0.1%	
DSS	527	69	14	437	7
	5.4%	13.1%	2.7%	82.9%	1.3%
		34.0%	0.8%	5.9%	2.0%
RSPCA	25	4	0.0%	21	0.0%
	0.3%	16.0%	0.0%	84.0%	0.0%
		2.0%		0.3%	
DTI	37	1	1	34	1
	0.4%	2.7%	2.7%	91.9%	2.7%
		0.5%	0.1%	0.5%	0.3%
Trading Standards	33	26	4	3	0.0%
	0.3%	78.8%	12.1%	9.1%	0.0%
		12.8%	0.2%	0.0%	
Education Welfare	118	11	16	91	0.0%
	1.2%	9.3%	13.6%	77.1%	0.0%
		5.4%	0.9%	1.2%	
British Waterways	10	0.0%	3	7	0.0%
	0.1%	0.0%	30.0%	70.0%	0.0%
			0.2%	0.1%	
BT Security	4	0.0%	0.0%	4	0.0%
	0.0%	0.0%	0.0%	100.0%	0.0%
				0.1%	
Inland Revenue	210	0.0%	1	208	1
	2.2%	0.0%	0.5%	99.0%	0.5%
			0.1%	2.8%	0.3%
Customs & Excise	123	2	1	120	0.0%
	1.3%	1.6%	0.8%	97.6%	0.0%
		1.0%	0.1%	1.6%	
HSE	15	6	2	7	0.0%
	0.2%	40.0%	13.3%	46.7%	0.0%
		3.0%	0.1%	0.1%	

SW Trains	271	0.0%	2	269	9
	2.8%	0.0%	0.7%	95.9%	3.3%
			0.1%	3.5%	2.6%
Cab Law Enforcement	6	0.0%	0.0%	6	0.0%
	0.1%	0.0%	0.0%	100.0%	0.0%
				0.1%	
London Buses	427	0.0%	0.0%	402	25
	4.4%	0.0%	0.0%	94.1%	5.9%
				5.4%	7.2%
Dept. of Health	1	0.0%	0.0%	1	0.0%
	0.0%	0.0%	0.0%	100.0%	0.0%
				0.0%	
Borough/County	3,989	17	365	3,424	183
Councils	41.2%	0.4%	9.2%	85.8%	4.6%
		8.4%	21.1%	46.2%	53.0%
Ministry of	1	0.0%	0.0%	1	0.0%
Agriculture	0.0%	0.0%	0.0%	100.0%	0.0%
				0.0%	

Appendix 3

Magistrates' Clerks Questionnaire

For each statement please circle the number which shows how strongly you agree or disagree.

1	2	3	4	5
disagree strongly	disagree a little	undecided	agree a little	agree strongly

1) The enforcement of the relevant parts of the criminal law is fulfilled satisfactorily by non-police prosecuting agencies.

    1   2   3   4   5

2) Non-police prosecutions are an efficient way of securing general compliance with the legislation.

    1   2   3   4   5

3) There is a social importance of the function and powers they possess.

    1   2   3   4   5

4) Although the investigative and prosecutorial roles in non-police agency cases is often performed by the same organisation, the system works well.

    1   2   3   4   5

5) There is a marked contrast between the police approach and that of the agencies in relation to investigation and prosecution of offences.

    1   2   3   4   5

6) The level of resources available to non-police agencies to investigate and prosecute is adequate.

      1   2   3   4   5

7) Non-police prosecutions contribute significantly to magistrate courts' work-loads.

      1   2   3   4   5

8) Non-police prosecutions are increasing significantly.

      1   2   3   4   5

9) Non-police prosecutions are decreasing significantly.

      1   2   3   4   5

10) The prosecutions currently undertaken by non-police agencies would be better dealt with as administrative offences outside the criminal justice system.

      1   2   3   4   5

Please include any further comments below.

Data Collection System

Prosecution Questionnaire

Q1   Which Court is the information from?

     Horseferry Road.. . ...☐

     Milton Keynes . ...☐

     Newcastle Under Lyme ....☐

Q2   Who was the prosecutor?

     DT /DVLA............☐ Go to question 3

     Vehicle Inspectorate........☐ Go to question 4

     TVLEO ....☐ Go to question 5

     Environment Agency ....☐ Go to question 6

     Electricity.... ....☐ Go to question 7

     DSS......... ....☐ Go to question 8

     RSPCA................☐ Go to question 9

     DTI..... ....☐ Go to question 10

     Trading Standards........ . .☐ Go to question 11

     Education Welfare. ... .☐ Go to question 12

     British Waterways ☐ Go to question 13

     B T Security..... .☐ Go to question 14

     Inland Revenue ...☐ Go to question 15

     Customs and excise ... .☐ Go to question 16

     HSE...... ....☐ Go to question 17

     S W Trains ....☐ Go to question 18

     Cab Law Enforcement........☐ Go to question 19

     London Buses......☐ Go to question 20

     Dept of Health .....☐ Go to question 21

     Borough/County Councils..............☐ Go to question 22

     Ministry of Agriculture......... .☐ Go to question 23

Q3   Offences prosecuted by the DT / DVLA.

     Driver and vehicle licence offences. ....☐

     No trade / good's operators licence .... ..☐

     Obstructing a police officer ....☐

     Other ....☐

Q4   Offences prosecuted by the Vehicle Inspectorate

     Gross weight Excess... ....☐

     Tachometer irregularities . ...☐

     No good's operators licence .. ..☐

     Forging a test certificate....................☐

     Failing to observe a statutory break ....☐

     Failing to produce a record sheet....... ..☐

     Ministry plate not affixed......... .. ..☐

     Test date disc not affixed.............. ....☐

     Obstructing a public entrance......... ..☐

     Other ....☐

Q5   Offences prosecuted by TVLEO

     No television licence. ....☐

     Other .. ..☐

Q6   Offences prosecuted by the Environment Agency

     Fishing without a rod licence. ....☐

Q7   Offences prosecuted by Electricity Supply Companies

     Breach of Road Traffic Regulations.. ......☐

Q8   Offences prosecuted by the DSS

     Dishonestly obtaining benefit ....☐

     Dishonestly obtaining a jobseekers allowance ....☐

     Aiding and abetting one who dishonestly obtained monies by deception...............☐

     Aiding and abetting the making of a false passport........... ....☐

     False accounting.................................☐

Q9   Offences prosecuted by RSPCA

     Causing unnecessary suffering to an animal......... ....☐

Q10 Offences prosecuted by DTI
    Obtaining credit while a bankrupt .. .. ☐
    Business trading offences while a
    bankrupt...................... ... . ☐
    Failing to disclose a loan when in
    voluntary liquidation..................... .. .. ☐
    Failing to produce documents for
    inspection required under Companies
    Act 1985 .... ☐
    Emitting noise amounting to a statutory
    nuisance .... ☐
    Acting as insolvency practitioner when
    not qualified to act .... ☐
    Accruing gambling losses to increase
    extent of insolvency .... ☐
    Other .... ☐

Q11 Offences prosecuted by DTS
    Making false trade description of goods . ☐
    Making a misleading advertisement of
    services provided..... .... ☐
    Removing 'sell by' date from goods........ ☐
    Failing to remove sheep's carcass
    without undue delay .... ☐
    Selling counterfeit goods..... .... ☐
    Other .... ☐

Q12 Offences prosecuted by Education Welfare
    Failing to ensure a child attends school
    regularly................. .... ☐

Q13 Offences prosecuted by British Waterways Board
    Keeping a pleasure boat without licence
    on canal/river...................... .... ☐

Q14 Offences prosecuted by BT Security
    Theft of monies............ .... ☐

Q15 Offences prosecuted by Inland Revenue
    Failing to pay sum recoverable as a civil
    debt .... ☐
    Other .... ☐

Q16 Offences prosecuted by Customs & Excise
    Intent to defraud HM of duty payable on
    excise goods........................... .... ☐
    Importing goods not 'for own use' . ... ☐
    Importing prohibited drugs .... ☐
    Other .... ☐

Q17 Offences prosecuted by HSE
    Offences under HSWA 1974. . ... ☐
    As an employer being uninsured .... ☐
    Other .... ☐

Q18 Offences prosecuted by S W Trains
    Intending to avoid payment of fare......... ☐
    Other .... ☐

Q19 Offences prosecuted by Cab Law Enforcement
    Being guilty of misbehaviour as a cab
    driver..... .... ☐
    Failing to wear badge conspicuously ...... ☐
    Leaving vehicle unlawfully .... ☐
    Plying cab for hire contrary to licence..... ☐
    Other .... ☐

Q20 Offences prosecuted by London Buses
    Intending to avoid payment of fare......... ☐
    Assault................. .... ☐
    Disorderly conduct .... ☐
    Other .... ☐

Q21 Dept of Health
    Possessing a product intended to be
    placed on market without authorisation .. ☐

Q22 Offences prosecuted by Borough/County Councils

Non- payment of Council Tax..... .... ☐

Breach of planning control . ... ☐

Offences under Environment Protection Act 1990 .... ☐

Offences under Clean Air Act 1993 .... ☐

Failing to remove and dispose of dog faeces................. .... ☐

Parking offences...................... .... ☐

Offences under Road Traffic Act/ Regs . ☐

Selling bone in beef .... ☐

Offences under Food Safety Act / Regs. ☐

Using premises without or not in accordance with licence .... ☐

Willfully obstructing free passage along a highway.. ☐

No street trading licence .... ☐

Displaying an advertisement without consent.. ☐

Supplying a video with no classification certification .... ☐

Carrying on work outside specified hours..................................... ... . ☐

Displaying a card in telephone kiosk ..... ☐

Retaining skip/scaffolding on highway without permission . ... ☐

Selling food unfit for human consumption . ... ☐

Selling food not of nature demanded. . . ☐

Placing a product on market without permission . ... ☐

Failing to declare an interest in premises...... .... ☐

Committing surgery under anaesthesia in an unregistered clinic .... ☐

Failing to state business name on fax .... ☐

Supplying fireworks to a person under eighteen... ☐

Misleading customers as to price of goods.. . . ☐

Failing to display corporate name.......... ☐

Offering goods for sale contrary to Trade Marks Act 1994................. .... ☐

Offering goods for sale contrary to Trade Description Act 1968 .... ☐

Accepting payment contrary to Accommodations Agencies Act 1953 ..... ☐

Transmitting noise amounting to a statutory nuisance...... .. .. ☐

Employing an unregistered door supervisor................. .... ☐

Failing to comply with a Council Notice.. ☐

Exposing employees to risk to safety ..... ☐

Q23 Offences prosecuted by the Ministry of Agriculture

Falsifying an expenses claim form .... ☐

Q24 What was the plea?

Guilty......... . .. . ☐

Not guilty .. .. ☐

Guilty MCA .. .. ☐

Not guilty MCA .... ☐

No appearance . ... ☐

Not known... ☐

N/A......... .... ☐

Q25 Verdict

Convicted / Proved . ... ☐

Not guilty .... ☐

Withdrawn / Dismissed.............. .... ☐

Adjourned .... ☐

Warrant issued for arrest.............. .... ☐

Summons not served .... ☐

Remanded in custody .... ☐

Remanded on bail................................ ... ☐

Emergency prohibition order .... ☐

Q26 If convicted what was the disposal?

Fine .... ☐

Remanded on bail.................................. ☐

Remanded in custody .... ☐

Imprisonment........... .... ☐

Probation .... ☐

Community Service .... ☐

Combination order .. .. ☐

Absolute discharge........ .... ☐

Conditional discharge .... ☐

Sentence suspended............................. ☐

Q27 Was the 'accused' present in court?

Yes .... ☐

No... .... ☐

Not known... ☐

N/A .. . . ☐

Q28 Was the 'accused' represented in court?

Yes .... ☐

No.... .... ☐

Not known................ .. .. ☐

N/A . ... ☐

Bibliography

Annual Report of Her Majesty's Chief Inspector of the Magistrates' Court Service 1998/99 (1999), London: The Stationery Office.

Ashworth, A. (1975), 'Reason, Logic and Criminal Liability', 91 LQR 102.

Ashworth, A. (1981), 'The Elasticity of Mens Rea', in C. Tapper (ed.), *Crime, Proof and Punishment*, London: Butterworths.

Ashworth, A. (1995), *Sentencing and Criminal Justice*, London: Butterworths.

Ashworth, A. (1999), *Principles of Criminal Law*, Oxford: Oxford University Press.

Baldwin, J. (1974), 'The Role of Victim in Certain Property Offences', *Criminal Law Review*, pp. 353–8.

Baldwin, J. and McConville, M. (1977), *Negotiated Justice*, London: Martin Robertson.

Bardach, E. and Kagan, R. (1982), *Going by the Book: The problem of regulatory unreasonableness*, Philadelphia: Temple University Press.

Barnett, H. (1992) 'Hazardous Waste, Distributional Conflict and a Trilogy of Failures', *Journal of Human Justice*, 3 (2), pp. 93–110.

Bentham, J. (1975), *The Theory of Legislation*, New York: Oceana.

Black, J. (1997), *Rules and Regulators*, Oxford: Clarendon Press.

Blackstone, W. (1979 [1769]), *Commentaries on the Laws of England*, facsimile of 1st edn, Chicago: University of Chicago Press.

Bottoms, A.E. and McClean, J.D. (1976), *Defendants in the Criminal Process*, London: Routledge.

Carson, W.G. (1970a), 'White Collar Crime and the Enforcement of Factory Legislation', *British Journal of Criminology*, 10, pp. 383–98.

Carson, W.G. (1970b), 'Some Sociological Aspects of Strict Liability and the Enforcement of Factory Legislation', *Modern Law Review*, 33, July, pp. 396–412.

Cassels, J. (1993), *The Uncertain Promise of Law*, Toronto: University of Toronto Press.

Cohen, S. (1985), *Visions of Social Control*, London: Polity.

Cranston, R. (1979), *Regulating Business*, London: Macmillan.

Cranston, R. (1985) *Consumers and the Law*, London: Butterworths.

Davies, M., Croall, H. and Tyrer, J. (1995), *Criminal Justice. An introduction to the criminal justice system in England and Wales*, London: Longman.

Devlin, P. (1960), *The Criminal Prosecution in England*, London: Oxford University Press.

Diamond, S. (1971) 'The Rule of Law Versus the Order of Custom', in C.E. Reasons, *Sociology of Law: A conflict perspective*, London: Butterworths.

Dickens, B.M. (1970), 'Discretion in Local Authority Prosecutions', *Criminal Law Review*, pp. 618–33.

Dickens, B.M. (1974), *The Prosecuting Roles of the Attorney-General and the Director of Public Prosecutions*, Public Law, pp. 50–73.

Durkheim, E. (1984 [1893]), *The Division of Labour in Society*, London: Macmillan.

Edwards, J. (1964), *The Law Officers of the Crown*, London: Sweet and Maxwell.

Engels, F. (1969 [1845]), *The Condition of the Working Class in England*, London: Panther.

Field, S. and Jorg, N. (1991), 'Corporate Liability and Manslaughter: Should we be going Dutch?', *Criminal Law Review*, pp. 156–71.

Foucault, M. (1979), *Discipline and Punish*, trans. A. Sheridan, Harmondsworth: Penguin.

Garland, D. (1990), *Punishment and Modern Society*, Oxford: Oxford University Press.

Hadden, T. (1968), *The Control of Company Food*, London: PEP Pamphlet.

Hadden, T. (1977), *Company Law and Capitalism*, London, Weidenfeld.

Hall, J. (1952), *Theft, Law and Society*, New York: Bobbs Merrill.

Harding, A. (1966), *A Social History of England*, Harmondsworth: Penguin.

Hart, H.L.A. (1961), *The Concept of Law*, Oxford: Clarendon Press.

Hay, D., Linebaugh, P., Thompson, E.P. and Winslow, C. (eds) (1975), *Albion's Fatal Tree*, Harmondsworth: Penguin.

Health and Safety Executive (1985), *Measuring the Effectiveness of HSE Field Activities. HSE Occasional Paper 11*, London: HMSO.

Hillyard P. and Sim, J. (1997), 'The Political Economy of Socio-Legal Research', in Thomas, P. (ed.), *Socio-Legal Studies*, Aldershot: Dartmouth, pp. 45–75.

Holdsworth, W. (1936), *A History of English Law*, Vol. II, London: Methuen & Co.

Hutter, B.M. (1988), *The Reasonable Arm of the Law? The Law Enforcement Procedures of Environmental Health Officers*, Oxford: Clarendon.

Jackson, R.M. (1967), *Enforcing the Law*, London, Macmillan.

JUSTICE (1970), *The Prosecution Process in England and Wales*, London: Stevens.

JUSTICE (1979), *Pre-Trial Criminal Procedure: Police Powers and the Prosecution Process*, London: JUSTICE.

Kagan, R. (1984), 'On Regulatory Inspectorates and Police', in K. Hawkins and J. Thomas (eds), *Enforcing Regulation*, Boston: Kluwer-Hijhoff, pp. 38–64.

Kiralfy, A. (1958), *Outlines of English Legal History*, London: Sweet & Maxwell.

Lacey, N. (1988), *State Punishment: Political Principles and Community Values*, London: Routledge.

Lacey, N. and Wells, C. (1998), *Reconstructing Criminal Law*, London: Butterworths.

Law Commission (1997), *Consents to Prosecution*, Consultation Paper No. 149, London: HMSO.

Law Commission (1998), *Consents to Prosecution* (Law Com. No. 255), London: HMSO.

Lidstone, K.W., Hogg, R. and Sutcliffe, F. (1980), *Prosecutions by Private Individuals and Non-Police Agencies*, London: HMSO.

Lord Chancellor's Department (1998), *The Future Role of the Justices' Clerk*, London: LCD.

Maguire, M. (1994), 'Crime Statistics, Patterns, and Trends: Changing perceptions and their implications', in M. Maguire et al. (eds), *The Oxford Handbook of Criminology*, Oxford: Oxford University Press, pp. 233–91.

Marx, K. and Engels, F. (1970 [1845]), 'The German Ideology', in *Selected Works*, Vol. III, Moscow: Progress.

Mawby, R. (1978), 'Crime and Law Enforcement in Different Residential Areas of the City of Sheffield', unpublished doctoral thesis, University of Sheffield.

Mawby, R. (1979), 'Policing by the Post Office', *British Journal of Criminology*, 19, pp. 242–53.

Milsom, S.F.C. (1981), *Historical Foundations of the Common Law*, London: Butterworths.

Nelken, D. (1987), 'Critical Criminal Law', *Journal of Law and Society*, Vol. 14, No. 1, Spring, p. 105.

Nelken, D. (1990), 'Why Punish?', *The Modern Law Review*, 53, pp. 829–34.

Norrie, A. (1993), *Crime, Reason and History*, London: Butterworths.

North Staffordshire Magistrates' Courts Committee (1998/9), Annual Report.

Pashukanis, E.B. (1978 [1924]), *Law and Marxism – A General Theory*, London: Pluto Press.

Radzinowicz, L. (1948), *A History of English Criminal Law*, Vol. 1, London: Stevens.

Reiner, R. (1996), 'The Case of the Missing Crimes', in R. Levitas and W. Guy (eds), *Interpreting Official Statistics*, London: Routledge, pp. 185–205.

RoSPA (1998), *Managing Occupational Road Risk*, Birmingham: The Royal Society for the Prevention of Accidents.

Royal Commission on Environmental Pollution (1995), *Eighteenth Report. Transport and the Environment*, Oxford: Oxford University Press.

Rutherford, A. (1993), *Criminal Justice and the Pursuit of Decency*, Oxford: Oxford University Press.

Sanders, A. (1997), 'Criminal Justice: The development of criminal justice research in Britain', in P. Thomas (ed.), *Socio-Legal Studies*, Aldershot: Dartmouth, pp. 185–205.

SCETRA (1999), *The Work of the Health and Safety Committee*, HC828, London: HMSO.

Sharpe, J.A. (1984), *Crime in Early Modern Britain 1550–1750*, London: Longman.

Sigler, J.A. (1974), 'Public Prosecutions in England and Wales', *Criminal Law Review*, pp. 642–51.

Smith, J.C. and Hogan, B. (1996), *Criminal Law*, London: Butterworths.

Stafford, R.J. (1989), *Private Prosecutions*, London: Shaw & Sons.

Stein, P. (1984), *Legal Institutions*, London: Butterworths.

Taylor, P. (Lord Taylor of Gosforth, Lord Chief Justice) (1993), 'What do we Want from our Judges?', text delivered as 17th Leggett Lecture, 26 November, University of Surrey.

Thompson, E.P. (1975), *Whigs and Hunters*, Harmondsworth: Penguin.
Wilcox, A.F. (1972), *The Decision to Prosecute*, London: Butterworths.
Williams, G. (1983), *Textbook of Criminal Law*, London: Stephens.
Zander, M. and Glasser, C. (1967), 'A Study in Representation', *New Law Journal*, 117, pp. 815–17.

Index